D1314199

Delicious Dishes,

Jamie
+ Lana

ENTERTAINING IN STYLE

Inspired Recipes + Kitchen Tips
+
Delicious Dishes

JAMIE GWEN + LANA SILLS

ENTERTAINING IN STYLE

Inspired Recipes + Kitchen Tips + Delicious Dishes

Whether you're planning festive gatherings or simple dinners, you can make every occasion special. *Entertaining In Style* features inspired recipes and menus for breakfast, brunch, lunch, Sunday suppers, family feasts and holiday parties. With the beauty of HSN's Infusion Brands Triple Burner, Chef Jamie Gwen and Lana Sills share recipes for grand buffets throughout the year.

With creative and flavorful ideas, along with kitchen tips and entertaining advice, you can delight hungry family and friends with fabulous food, all from your Triple Burner. *Entertaining In Style* is the essential cookbook for at-home entertaining, potluck parties, family festivities and delicious meals.

Jamie Gwen & Lana Sills

ENTERTAINING IN STYLE

Jamie Gwen and Lana Sills

Visit www.chefjamie.com for more mouthwatering recipes, lessons and kitchen tips for Entertaining In Style.

Copyright © 2016 Jamie Gwen and Lana Sills
ISBN-13: 978-0-9816941-2-2

Published by Tastebud Entertainment, Inc.

Food photography provided by Lisenbee Photography, Lana Sills and Jamie Gwen

Book design by Brett Burner, Lamp Post

Printed in the USA

This book is dedicated to all the great cooks who live to eat. After many years of great success offering the Triple Burner Buffet on HSN, we've compiled this collection of recipes that can all be made using your amazing Triple Burner. The recipes can be adapted for the stovetop and many dishes are baked in the oven, but they all work beautifully on a buffet!

We know that your next party or gathering will be scrumptious and successful!

Cheers to celebrations~

JAMIE + LANA

BUFFET ESSENTIALS

Buffets are a wonderful way to host a party, where you can create a dining experience that tempts everyone and allows you time to mingle and enjoy! Whether it's a sumptuous Spring Buffet, Summer Bash, Fall Potluck or hearty Winter Feast, your friends will be delighted by delicious dishes and they'll keep coming back for more. Your culinary victories will be rooted in good planning and thoughtfulness.

A beautiful, abundant buffet makes any event a celebration. Everyone loves an Italian Buffet with a trio of pastas to choose from or an informal buffet where everyone can enjoy a night filled with great conversation. And, a dessert buffet is a sweet way to end an evening with friends. We like to create our menus around a theme or holiday and gather friends and family to celebrate!

For Stress-Free Entertaining...

- Plan for 3 drinks per guest and 1 pound of ice per person (this allows for melting!).

- You will get six glasses from a standard-size bottle of wine or Champagne.

- Count on 4 to 6 hors d'oeuvres per person if you're serving a main course. If you're serving only cocktails and hors d'oeuvres, plan on 10 to 12 tastes per person.

- Plan on ¼ of a pound of meat per person and 1 cup of salad, vegetables, pasta or rice.

- Don't neglect the vegetarians. Offer a vegetable-forward dish on your buffet, like veggie fried rice or a primavera pasta.

- Consider the big picture. To impress your guests, transform your buffet table by using vases filled with tall florals or add candles to add light and dimension. Make risers using empty boxes or books of different heights, and drape a large tablecloth over the risers. Play with texture and color.

CONTENTS

THE MAIN DISH • 63

ON THE SIDE • 91

PASTA + RICE • 107

SOMETHING SWEET • 127

DRINKS + SIPS • 151

BREAKFAST

+

BRUNCH

EGGS POACHED in a
RICH TOMATO SAUCE

SERVES 4

This poached egg dish makes a terrific breakfast, brunch or a quick dinner! Serve the eggs over toasted bread with the tomato sauce and steamed spinach or kale on the side. You can add a dollop of ricotta or goat cheese when serving, if you like.

1 tablespoon good quality olive oil
2 garlic cloves, minced or grated
1 teaspoon granulated sugar
   Pinch of red pepper flakes
1 28-ounce jar store-bought
   marinara sauce

4 large eggs
   Salt and freshly ground pepper
4 slices toasted country or French
   bread, for serving
   Grated Parmesan cheese, for
   serving

Heat the olive oil in a 3-quart pot over medium-high heat. Add the garlic and red pepper flakes and cook for 30 seconds, stirring often, until the garlic is lightly golden. Add the marinara sauce, season with salt and pepper and bring to a boil. Reduce the heat and simmer for 15 minutes.

Gently crack the eggs into the tomato sauce, cover the pot with a lid and let cook for 5 minutes. Remove from the heat and let stand for 3 minutes, uncovered. Place each egg onto a piece of toast and spoon the sauce over the eggs. Finish with the Parmesan cheese.

EASY BAKED BRIOCHE
FRENCH TOAST

SERVES 6

Somewhere between traditional French toast and bread pudding and so easy to prepare the night before! Serve it with fresh berries and peaches or in the Fall with caramelized apples and cranberry sauce.

---

1   24-ounce brioche loaf, cut into 1-inch cubes
1   8-ounce package cream cheese, cut into small cubes
¾   cup chopped pecans or walnuts
½   cup golden raisins, dried cranberries or dried blueberries
6   large eggs
2   cups whole milk
½   cup firmly packed dark brown sugar
2   teaspoons pure vanilla extract
1   teaspoon ground cinnamon
     Pinch of nutmeg
     Powdered sugar
     Grade B pure maple syrup, warmed

Generously butter a 3-quart pot. Place half of the bread cubes in a single layer in the pot, filling in all the gaps. Evenly scatter the cream cheese cubes, nuts and raisins on top. Cover completely with the remaining bread cubes.

In a large mixing bowl, whisk together the eggs, milk, brown sugar, vanilla, cinnamon and nutmeg. Pour the egg mixture over the bread cubes. Gently press down on the bread cubes to allow the top layer of bread to absorb the liquid. Cover with plastic wrap and refrigerate for four hours or overnight.

Preheat the oven to 350°F. Remove the pot from the refrigerator and let it sit at room temperature for 20 minutes. Bake the French Toast covered for 20 minutes, then uncover and bake 15 to 20 minutes longer, or until the cubes are nicely toasted and there's no liquid on the bottom of the pot. Let rest 10 minutes before serving.

Spoon the French Toast into bowls and finish with powdered sugar and warm maple syrup.

BREAKFAST CHILAQUILES

SERVES 4

Eggs, tortillas and cheese...what a wonderful way to start the day! Pantry items that can be put together quickly make up this traditional Mexican dish. Use up leftover corn tortillas and salsas and garnish with crema, shredded queso fresco, chopped red onion and avocado slices.

3	tablespoons corn oil
6	white corn tortillas, cut into ½-inch strips
4	large eggs, beaten
1	4-ounce can diced fire-roasted green chilies
½	teaspoon ground cumin
½	teaspoon dried oregano
½	cup shredded Monterey Jack cheese
2	tablespoons freshly chopped cilantro
1	cup of your favorite salsa
	Mexican Crema
	Hot Sauce

Heat the oil until almost smoking in a 3-quart pot. Add the tortilla strips and sauté until fragrant and beginning to crisp. Add the beaten eggs, chilies, cumin and oregano and cook until the eggs are just set. Mix in the cheese and cook until melted. Finish with cilantro, salsa and crema and pass hot sauce at the table.

APPLE-GLAZED SAUSAGES

SERVES 6

Whether you are serving eggs, grits, crispy waffles or French toast, these apple-glazed sausages are the ideal side dish. The apple juice, apple jelly and maple syrup create a delicious glaze that coats the sausages until they glisten with flavor. We recommend using smoked chicken sausage, turkey sausage, kielbasa or your favorite links.

2 pounds smoked sausage of your choice, sliced ½-inch thick
¼ cup apple juice
¼ cup apple jelly
¼ cup Grade B pure maple syrup

Heat the olive oil in a 3-quart pot over medium heat. Add the sliced sausage and cook, stirring often, for 5 minutes, or until the sauce is golden brown. Add the apple juice, apple jelly and maple syrup and simmer for 5 minutes, or until the sauce has thickened and the sausages are glazed.

TURKEY, APPLE + POTATO HASH

SERVES 4

We think of this as a year-round Hash using leftover roasted meats, pork chops, corned beef, chicken or bacon. Top it with a poached egg or finish with rich Southern gravy.

1	20-ounce bag frozen hash brown potatoes, thawed
4	cups cooked leftover turkey, diced
1	green apple – cored, seeded and diced
3	tablespoons freshly chopped parsley
⅓	cup low-sodium chicken broth
3	tablespoons heavy whipping cream
½	teaspoon ground sage
	Salt and freshly ground pepper
¼	cup vegetable oil

Combine the thawed hash browns, turkey, apple, parsley, chicken broth, cream and sage in a large mixing bowl. Season liberally with salt and pepper and mix well.

Heat a large sauté pan over medium heat. Add the oil and heat until almost smoking. Add the potato mixture and spread evenly in the pan. Cover the pan and cook for 15 minutes, stirring occasionally. Remove the lid, increase the heat to high and cook the hash for an additional 10 minutes or until crisp and golden brown.

PULL-APART CARAMEL COFFEE CAKE

SERVES 8

Imagine the best cinnamon roll you have ever tasted! This ooey, gooey caramel monkey bread is ready in just about an hour and deliciously rich. Add a vanilla glaze of confectioners sugar, heavy cream and vanilla for true heaven!

For the Caramel

1 ¼ cups packed dark brown sugar
12 tablespoons (1 ½ sticks) unsalted butter
1 teaspoon ground cinnamon
1 teaspoon pure vanilla extract
A generous pinch of salt

For the Coffee Cake

3 (7.5-ounce) tubes refrigerated buttermilk biscuits
8 tablespoons (1 stick) unsalted butter
½ cup granulated sugar
2 teaspoons ground cinnamon

Preheat the oven to 350°F. Butter a 3-quart casserole.

Combine the brown sugar, butter and cinnamon in a small saucepot and bring to a boil. Cook for 1 minute, stirring constantly. Remove from the heat and stir in the vanilla extract and salt.

Cut each biscuit in half and gently roll each piece of dough into a ball. Melt the butter in a medium-sized mixing bowl. In a separate bowl, stir together the granulated sugar and cinnamon. Drop a few balls of dough at a time into the melted butter and coat well. Drop each dough ball into the cinnamon sugar mixture and toss to coat. Shake off any excess and layer the balls, about ½-inch apart, in the prepared pan in a single layer. Pour half of the caramel over the dough balls. Repeat using the remaining dough balls, staggering the balls to create the pull-apart effect after baking. Pour the remaining caramel over the second layer of biscuit dough.

Bake for 20 to 25 minutes or until golden brown. Remove the coffee cake from the oven and cool for 5 minutes before inverting onto a plate.

MAPLE BERRY BAKED OATMEAL

SERVES 6

Your favorite childhood flavors are in this healthy oatmeal! Here is our recipe for the perfect breakfast. Have you even seen purple oatmeal? When the berries break down during cooking they will turn the oatmeal purplish red and add great flavor. Swirl in some vanilla yogurt and your favorite toasted nuts. You will love every bite!

---

1 cup chopped pecans
4 cups old-fashioned oats
3 teaspoons baking powder
1 teaspoon ground cinnamon
½ teaspoon salt
3 cups whole milk, almond milk or coconut milk
⅓ cup Grade B pure maple syrup
3 tablespoons unsalted butter, melted
3 large eggs
2 teaspoons pure vanilla extract
4 cups of mixed berries
   (blueberries, blackberries, sliced strawberries)
2 tablespoons turbinado sugar

Preheat the oven to 375°F. Butter a 3-quart pot.

Place the pecans on a baking sheet and roast in the oven for 5 minutes, or until fragrant and toasted.

In a mixing bowl, combine the oats, toasted pecans, baking powder, cinnamon and salt. Add the milk, maple syrup, melted butter, eggs, and vanilla. Whisk well to blend. Gently stir in the berries.

Pour the mixture into the prepared saucepot. Top with the turbinado sugar. Bake uncovered for 40 to 45 minutes, or until the oatmeal is golden on top and tender.

STARTERS

+

SNACKS

BAKED BRIE
with a COMPOTE of FRUIT

SERVES 8

1 cup pitted dried dates, chopped
1 green apple – peeled, cored and chopped
1 ripe pear – peeled, cored and chopped
½ cup currants or raisins
1 cup chopped pecans
1 cup dry white wine or apple juice
1 16-ounce wheel of Brie cheese, well chilled
   Crackers and/or French bread slices

Combine the dates, apple, pear, currants, pecans and wine in a 3-quart pot over medium heat. Bring to a boil, then reduce to a simmer and cook for 10 minutes or until the fruit has plumped and absorbed most of the liquid. Remove the pot from the heat and let cool completely.

Preheat the oven to 350°F. Place the whole Brie on an aluminum foil-lined baking sheet. Slice the Brie horizontally into two halves. Place the bottom half of the Brie, cut side up, in a shallow round baking dish. Spread the Brie with three-quarters of the fruit mixture. Cover with the top half of the Brie, cut side down. Spoon the remaining fruit onto the top of the Brie.

Bake the Brie for 25 to 30 minutes or until the cheese melts at the edges and the center is warm. Serve with crackers or bread.

CHEDDAR BEER DIP
with SOFT PRETZELS

SERVES 8

Bring on game day with this warm and hearty dip made with beer and lots of cheddar cheese. Add a few dashes of hot sauce or a squeeze of Sriracha and warm the soft pretzels with a brush of butter and everything bagel seasoning!

---

1   cup Pale Ale
4   cups shredded cheddar cheese
3   tablespoons unsalted butter
3   tablespoons all-purpose flour
4   cups whole milk
1   teaspoon freshly squeezed lemon juice
    Salt and freshly ground pepper
8   frozen soft pretzels, baked according to package directions

Pour the beer into a 3-quart pot and bring to a boil. Simmer until reduced by half.

In a separate 3-quart pot, combine the butter and flour. Cook over medium-low heat, stirring constantly, for 3 minutes. Add the reduced Pale Ale and the milk and continue to cook, whisking often, until the mixture is thickened, about 5 minutes.

Slowly whisk in the cheddar cheese until smooth and fully incorporated, then add the lemon juice, salt and pepper.

Serve the dip warm with soft pretzels that have been warmed.

GARLICKY FONTINA FONDUE

SERVES 4

Bubbling, cheesy and the perfect dip for a party. Dip cooked sausage, potatoes, asparagus, mushrooms and cubes of sourdough or dark rye bread. Slather some on a rare roast beef sandwich, pour some over sausages and grilled vegetable or swirl in some sun-dried tomato pesto! This cheesy, interactive dish is ready for a comeback and your guests will be buzzing about this pot of fondue.

---

3   cups shredded Fontina cheese
1   cup shredded Monterey jack cheese
2   tablespoons cornstarch
2   cups of your favorite Chardonnay
2   teaspoons minced garlic
¼   teaspoon freshly grated nutmeg
    Salt and freshly ground pepper

In a large mixing bowl, combine the two cheeses with the flour and toss to coat well. In a 3-quart saucepot, bring the wine and garlic to a simmer over medium-low heat. Add half of the cheese and whisk until melted. Add the remaining cheese and whisk until completely melted and combined. Season with salt, pepper and nutmeg and simmer until the mixture is smooth, about 2 minutes more.

Serve with slices of sausages, potatoes, vegetables and grilled labread for dipping.

HOT SPINACH + ARTICHOKE DIP

SERVES 6

A go-to appetizer for parties that is creamy inside and crispy on top. Serve with sliced jalapeños for the spicy crowd or diced crisp bacon and extra Parmesan on top.

2 cups marinated artichokes, drained
4 cups frozen spinach, thawed and drained
1 teaspoon garlic, minced or grated
1 cup shredded Romano cheese
⅔ cup shredded Parmesan cheese
1 cup shredded mozzarella cheese
½ cup sour cream
¼ cup mayonnaise
¼ cup heavy whipping cream
   Hot sauce

Preheat the oven to 400°F. Butter a 3-quart pot.

In a food processor, combine the artichokes and spinach and pulse until roughly chopped. Add the garlic, Romano cheese, Parmesan and mozzarella, sour cream, mayonnaise and heavy cream and keep pulsing until the ingredients are well blended. Add hot sauce to taste. Spoon the dip into the prepared pot and bake for 30 minutes or until the cheese is melted and the dip just starts to bubble.

Serve with tortilla chips for dipping and sour cream and salsa.

MARSALA MUSHROOM RAGOÛT

SERVES 6

Simple, sophisticated and scrumptious. We like to serve these mushrooms on slices of crunchy French baguette as an appetizer or on top of a steak with a drizzle of truffle oil. Or, spoon the mushroom ragout over a scoop of garlic mashed potatoes in a martini glass for an easy to eat buffet treat. Try using criminis, shitakes, oyster mushrooms, button mushrooms or a mix of domestic and exotic.

1	2-ounce bag dried shitake mushrooms
2	tablespoons unsalted butter
2	tablespoons good quality olive oil
2	shallots, minced
2	garlic cloves, minced or grated
4	cups white and crimini mushrooms, sliced
½	cup Marsala
2	teaspoons fresh thyme leaves, chopped
2	tablespoons freshly chopped chives
	Salt and freshly ground pepper

Place the dried mushrooms in a small heatproof bowl and cover with boiling water. Let stand for 10 minutes to reconstitute the mushrooms. Drain the mushrooms, discarding the soaking liquid, and trim the stems of the shitakes.

Combine the butter and oil in a 3-quart pot. Add the shallots and garlic and cook over medium-low heat until translucent, about 5 minutes. Increase the heat to medium-high and add the reconstituted dried mushrooms and the fresh mushrooms. Sauté, stirring often, until the mushroom liquid has evaporated, about 10 minutes. Add the red wine and simmer for 3 minutes, or until the wine is reduced to a glaze. Stir in the thyme and season with salt and pepper. Finish with chopped chives.

HOT CLAM DIP

SERVES 6

Simple to make, but tastes great! Make it your own by mixing in green chiles, salsa or fresh cilantro. This creamy family favorite is perfect for sitting and munching in front of a football game. Serve with a platter of crudites, pita chips or thick-cut potato chips. Serve with a platter of crudités, pita chips or thick cut potato chips.

---

4   8-ounce packages cream cheese, at room temperature
4   tablespoons finely grated sweet yellow onion
4   tablespoons good beer
3   teaspoons Worcestershire sauce
2   tablespoons fresh lemon juice
2   teaspoons hot sauce
4   6.5-ounce cans minced clams, drained
    Salt and freshly ground pepper
    Toasted Bread Cubes, Crackers, Chips and Veggies, for dipping

Preheat the oven to 350°F. In a mixing bowl, combine the cream cheese, onion, beer, Worcestershire sauce, lemon juice, hot pepper sauce, and salt. Blend well. Fold in the clams and mix well. Pour the clam dip into a 3-quart casserole and top with a lid.

Bake for 30 minutes or until heated through. Serve with toasted bread, crackers, chips and veggies.

SRIRACHA POPCORN

SERVES 6

Great for popcorn lovers and Sriracha lovers! It's spicy, salty, tangy, buttery and addictive.

1   tablespoon vegetable oil
¼   cup popcorn kernels
4   tablespoons unsalted butter, melted
2   tablespoons Sriracha
     Zest of 1 Lime
     Generous pinch of salt

Pour the oil into a 3-quart pot and add the popcorn kernels. Place over medium heat, cover with a lid and cook, shaking the pan often, until the popcorn pops completely.

Whisk together the melted butter, Sriracha, lime zest and salt in a mixing bowl. Drizzle over the warm popcorn in the pot and toss to coat.

SWEDISH MEATBALLS

SERVES 6 AS AN APPETIZER

One of the most popular traditional holiday recipes, you can serve these mini meatballs as an appetizer or spoon them over egg noodles for a family dinner. They're also the perfect addition to a Christmas office party.

For the Meatballs

- 4 tablespoons unsalted butter
- 1 tablespoon good quality olive oil
- 1 small sweet onion, chopped
- 2 slices day-old rye bread – crusts trimmed, torn into pieces
- ⅔ cup low-sodium beef broth
- 1 whole egg
- ¼ teaspoon ground allspice
- 1 ½ pound ground beef
- ½ pound ground pork
  Salt and freshly ground pepper

For the Sauce

- 2 tablespoons unsalted butter
- 2 tablespoons all-purpose flour
- 1 ⅓ cups low-sodium beef broth
- ⅓ cup heavy whipping cream
  Pinch of ground allspice
  Freshly chopped parsley

For the meatballs, melt 2 tablespoons butter with the olive oil in a 3-quart pot over medium heat. Add the onion and sauté until tender and beginning to caramelize, stirring often, about 15 minutes. Cool slightly. Combine the bread and beef broth in a large mixing bowl. Mix in the caramelized onion, egg, allspice and pepper. Add the ground beef and ground pork and season liberally with salt and pepper. Blend well.

Shape the meat mixture into 1-inch balls, being sure not to pack the meat too tightly. Melt the remaining 2 tablespoons of butter in a large skillet over medium heat. Add the meatballs and sauté until golden brown all over, about 10 minutes. Transfer the meatballs to a plate and keep warm.

For the sauce, melt the butter in a 3-quart pot. Add the flour to the drippings in the same skillet and stir over medium heat until brown, about 4 minutes. Add the beef broth and whisk until smooth, then add the cream. Simmer until the sauce is thick and smooth, stirring frequently, about 5 minutes. Season to taste with allspice, salt and pepper. Add the meatballs to the sauce and stir to coat. Cook for 3 minutes or until the meatballs are heated through. Finish with parsley.

SOUP

+

CHILI

SMOKED TOMATO SOUP

SERVES 4 TO 6

We smoke our tomatoes to create the deep, rich flavor for this satisfying soup. Using your steamer pot top over alderwood or mesquite chips scattered in the pot below, is a wonderful way to add smoky complexity to basic tomato soup. Place the cored, seeded, halved tomatoes in the steamer part of your pot, cover and smoke for approximately 20 to 30 minutes or until the tomatoes are soft. Add a few tablespoons of heavy cream and finish with a few toasted baguette slices with melted cheese floating on top! This divine smoky tomato soup is a wonderful base for a cold Gazpacho, too.

14   plum tomatoes – cut in half, cored and seeded
1   tablespoon unsalted butter
1   tablespoon good quality olive oil
½   small sweet yellow onion, minced
2   garlic cloves, minced or grated
3   cups low-sodium chicken broth or vegetable broth
2   tablespoons half & half, optional
    Salt and freshly ground pepper
    Baguette slices, toasted with melted Gruyere cheese

Cut the tomatoes in half and squeeze to remove the seeds. Place the wood chips in the bottom of a 3-quart pot. Place the tomato halves in the steamer insert and place the steamer on top of the pot. Cover with a lid and smoke the tomatoes on medium heat until the tomatoes are soft, about 20 to 30 minutes. Place the smoked tomatoes in the food processor and puree until smooth.

Heat the butter and olive oil in a 3-quart pot. Add the onions and garlic and sauté until translucent. Add the smoked tomato purée and the broth and simmer for 15 minutes. Add the half & half, if desired. Season with salt and freshly ground pepper.

CREAMY TOMATO BASIL SOUP
with GRILLED CHEESE CROUTONS

SERVES 4

Tomato soup always hits the spot especially when it's topped with grilled cheese croutons! Enjoy this warm filling soup on a cold night or for a light lunch. Add a few cloves of roasted garlic for delicious garlicky sweetness. It freezes well, so you can break out the taste of summer all year long!

2	tablespoons good quality olive oil	1	teaspoon granulated sugar
2	tablespoons unsalted butter	4	cups low-sodium chicken broth
2	medium yellow onions, diced	½	cup fresh basil leaves
2	garlic cloves, minced or grated	½	cup heavy whipping cream
1	28-ounce can crushed tomatoes		Salt and freshly ground pepper
2	tablespoons tomato paste		Grilled Cheese Croutons

Heat the olive oil and butter in a 3-quart pot over medium heat. Add the onions and cook over medium-low heat for 15 minutes, stirring occasionally, until golden brown. Add the garlic and cook for 1 minute more. Add the tomato paste and sugar and cook 3 minutes more. Stir in the crushed tomatoes, chicken broth and basil and season with salt and pepper. Bring the soup to a boil, then lower the heat and simmer for 15 minutes. Using an immersion blender, purée the soup until smooth.

Stir in the cream and the remaining tablespoon of butter, return the soup to a simmer and cook for 10 minutes more, stirring often. Serve hot with Grilled Cheese Croutons scattered on top.

GRILLED CHEESE CROUTONS

4	slices egg bread or brioche	1 ½	cups shredded cheese – Fontina,
3	tablespoons unsalted butter,		Monterey Jack or another good
	at room temperature		melting cheese of your choice

Heat a large sauté pan over medium heat. Place two slices of bread on a cutting board and divide the cheese between the tow slices. Top with the remaining bread slices, to form two sandwiches. Spread the softened butter on both sides of the exterior of each sandwich. Sauté the sandwiches for about 4 minutes on each side, or until nicely browned. Cut the sandwiches into 1-inch cubes to make croutons.

SMOKY MINESTRONE
with TORTELLINI

SERVES 6

There is so much veggie goodness in this hearty soup. We start with a little bit of bacon or pancetta for a smoky flavor. The smokiness of the bacon adds a depth of flavor to the tomato broth, with the added bonus of tortellini. Add the rind from a wedge of Parmesan while it's simmering, to increase deliciousness! Top with grated Parmesan and a dollop of pesto and serve with a salad of prosciutto and melon over arugula with Tiramisu for dessert.

3   tablespoons good quality olive oil
4   strips bacon, cut into small pieces
1   small sweet yellow onion, diced
1   garlic clove, minced
1   leek – cut in half, cleaned and sliced thinly
3   carrots, coarsely chopped
1   zucchini, thinly sliced
1   russet potato, peeled and diced
4   cups vegetable broth or low-sodium chicken broth

1   28-ounce can diced tomatoes in juice
1   15-ounce can cannellini beans, rinsed and drained
2   cups fresh baby spinach leaves or kale leaves
1   9-ounce package fresh cheese tortellini
½   cup freshly grated Parmesan cheese
    Salt & freshly ground pepper

Heat 1 tablespoon of olive oil in a 3-quart pot. Add the bacon and cook until the fat renders and the bacon is crispy. Remove the bacon from the pot using a slotted spoon and set aside.

Add the remaining 1 tablespoon of olive oil to the bacon grease and add the onion. Sauté, stirring often, until the onion is translucent, about 5 minutes. Add the garlic, leek, carrots, zucchini, potatoes, salt and pepper and sauté, stirring often, for 5 minutes. Add the broth and bring to a boil. Reduce the heat to low, cover the pot with a lid and simmer for 15 minutes, stirring occasionally. Add the diced tomatoes with their juice, beans, spinach and tortellini. Simmer 10 minutes more.

To serve, ladle the soup into soup bowls and finish with crispy bacon and Parmesan cheese.

SPLIT PEA SOUP...
SMOKY or SPICY

SERVES 4 TO 6

The spicy version is for the Chorizo lover and the smoky version uses a ham hock that is removed before puréeing the soup. This velvety soup will bring back childhood memories. Make a vegetarian version without the ham bone or chorizo. This soup tastes better the next day, and the day after that, and...

1	pound green split peas
10	cups low-sodium chicken broth
½	pound diced chorizo (or a small ham hock)
1	small sweet yellow onion, peeled and cut into quarters
2	carrots, peeled and chopped
1	celery stalk, chopped
1	garlic clove
1	bay leaf
	Salt and freshly ground pepper

Combine all of the ingredients in a 3-quart pot. Cover the pot with a lid and bring the soup to a boil, then reduce the heat to simmer and cook the soup until the peas are tender, about 1 hour.

Remove the pot from the heat and discard the bay leaf. Using an immersion blender, or in batches in your food processor, purée the soup until smooth. Adjust the seasoning and serve.

CUBAN BLACK BEAN SOUP

SERVES 4 TO 6

This soup is extremely easy and quick to prepare. A Cuban classic that is creamy and full of flavor. The lime juice gives it a little tang and your house will be filled with a wonderful aroma. Add more cumin and hot sauce to your taste. Serve over rice and garnish with diced raw onions and sour cream. We love the crunch of little bits of chopped chicharrónes on top!

2	tablespoons good quality olive oil
1	small sweet yellow onion, diced
3	garlic cloves, minced or grated
1	tablespoon fresh thyme, chopped
1	teaspoon ground cumin
½	teaspoon dried oregano
4	15-ounce cans black beans, drained
6	cups low-sodium chicken broth
1	14-ounce can diced tomatoes in juice
1	teaspoon hot sauce
2	teaspoons freshly squeezed lime juice
2	tablespoons cold unsalted butter

Heat the oil in a 3-quart pot over medium heat. Add the onion and sauté until tender and caramelized, about 10 minutes. Add the garlic, thyme, cumin and oregano and sauté 1 minute more.

Add the beans, broth, tomatoes with juice and hot sauce. Bring the soup to a boil, then reduce the heat to medium-low and simmer, stirring occasionally, for 20 minutes. Remove the soup from the heat and stir in the lime juice and cold butter.

Using an immersion blender, or in batches in your food processor, purée the soup until smooth. Adjust the seasoning and serve.

BACON CORN CHOWDER

SERVES 6

Rich with flavor and easy to put together. For a bit of zip, add shredded pepper jack cheese and chopped jalapeños. Serve with a veggie tray and hot rolls and look forward to leftovers!

½ pound thick-cut bacon, cut into 1-inch pieces
1 large sweet yellow onion, diced
1 small fennel bulb, trimmed and diced
1 red, orange or yellow bell pepper – seeded and diced
1 tablespoon all-purpose flour
3 sprigs fresh thyme
1 bay leaf
4 cups chicken broth or lobster stock
3 ears fresh corn, kernels cut from the cob or 2 cups frozen corn, defrosted
3 red new potatoes, diced
1 ½ cups half & half
Salt and freshly ground pepper
Freshly chopped parsley

Heat the olive oil in a 3-quart pot over medium heat. Add the bacon and cook until crisp. Remove the bacon with a slotted spoon and set aside. Add the onion and fennel to the bacon grease in the pot and sauté for 10 minutes, or until tender. Add the bell pepper and sauté 2 minutes more. Add the flour, thyme sprigs and bay leaf and stir to dissolve the flour. Add the broth or stock and bring to a simmer. Cook for 15 minutes to blend flavors, then add the corn kernels and potatoes and simmer 15 minutes more.

Remove the pot from the heat, remove the bay leaf and thyme sprigs and stir in the half and half. Adjust the seasoning to taste. Place half of the chowder in the blender and purée until smooth. Add the puréed mixture back to the corn chowder and stir to combine. Finish with parsley.

ASIAN TOFU NOODLE SOUP

SERVES 4

A simply delicious soup that goes from pot to table in 30 minutes or less. Customize the veggies to suit your preferences. Serve with ginger garlic rice or a noodle dish and vegetable spring rolls for a healthy meal.

---

2   ounces (about 1 cup) thin rice stick noodles
2   teaspoons sesame oil
2   garlic cloves, minced or grated
1   teaspoon freshly grated ginger
6   cups low-sodium chicken or vegetable broth
1   tablespoon low-sodium soy sauce
8   ounces firm tofu, diced
2   carrots, peeled and thinly sliced
1   cup small broccoli florets
1   cup snow peas
1   cup Napa cabbage, chopped
1   cup thinly sliced mixed mushrooms
1   cup bean sprouts
2   green onions, chopped
    Sriracha or Hot Sauce, for serving

Place the rice noodles in a mixing bowl; pour boiling water over the noodles and let soak until the noodles are tender, about 10 minutes. Drain and set aside.

Heat the sesame oil in a 3-quart pot over medium heat. Add the garlic and ginger and sauté for 2 minutes. Add the broth and soy sauce and bring the soup to a boil. Add the tofu, all the vegetables and the noodles and simmer uncovered for 5 minutes. Add the bean sprouts and green onions. Serve with Sriracha or hot sauce.

QUICK CLAM CHOWDER

SERVES 4 TO 6

This is the truly decadent version of a comforting classic. A quick and easy chowder to make in just 30 minutes using canned clams and plenty of bacon. Serve with crusty bread and a salad on a chilly evening.

1	teaspoon good quality olive oil
½	pound thick-cut bacon, cut into ½-inch pieces
1	medium sweet yellow onion, diced
3	celery stalks, diced
2	garlic cloves, minced or grated
2	tablespoons all-purpose flour
2	russet potatoes, peeled and diced
2	8-ounce bottles clam juice
2	6 ½-ounce cans chopped clams – drained, with juices reserved
1	cup water
1	cup heavy whipping cream
	Freshly ground pepper
¼	cup freshly chopped parsley

Heat the olive oil in a 3-quart pot. Add the bacon and sauté until it begins to brown and most of the fat is rendered. Drain off all but 2 tablespoons of the bacon grease. Add the onion, celery, garlic and flour to pot and sauté until onions are soft, about 5 minutes, stirring often. Add the potatoes, clam juice, reserved juices from chopped clams and water. Bring the mixture to a boil. Reduce the heat and simmer uncovered until the potatoes are tender, about 20 minutes. Add the clams and heavy cream to the pot and simmer for 5 minutes. Season with pepper. Finish with chopped parsley.

GREEK LEMON CHICKEN SOUP

SERVES 4

A classic Greek soup, also known as Avgolemono soup, takes chicken soup to a whole new level. Rich with a creamy egg and lemon chicken broth and your choice of rice, orzo or pastina. It makes a delicious satisfying dinner with the addition of a green salad. We think lemon juice makes all food taste lighter and brighter. Use a rotisserie chicken and low-salt chicken broth for a quick soup + salad dinner and garnish with a lemon slice and some parsley.

---

1 tablespoon good quality olive oil	½ cup orzo
1 small leek, cleaned and thinly sliced	½ cup freshly squeezed lemon juice
1 celery stalk, sliced ½-inch thick	2 large eggs
½ pound skinless, boneless chicken thighs	2 tablespoons freshly chopped dill
	Lemon halves, for serving
6 cups low-sodium chicken broth	Kosher salt, freshly ground pepper

Heat the oil in a 3-quart pot over medium heat. Add the leek and celery and cook, stirring often, until the vegetables are soft, about 5 minutes. Add the chicken thighs and the broth, season with salt and pepper and bring to a boil. Reduce the heat to a simmer, cover the pot and cook until the chicken is cooked through, about 15 to 20 minutes. Transfer the chicken to a plate, let cool, then shred the chicken into bite-size pieces.

Meanwhile, return the broth to a boil. Add the orzo and cook until al dente, about 10 minutes.

In a large mixing bowl, whisk together the lemon juice and eggs. Slowly ladle 1 cup of the hot broth from the pot into the egg mixture, whisking constantly. Pour the entire mixture back into the pot and stir well to blend. Stir in the shredded chicken and the dill and adjust the seasoning. Serve hot.

CHEF'S TIP: Leeks need a good cleaning because they are grown in sandy soil. Cut off the dark green top and trim to where the color is a pale green, then trim the root end. Slice the stalk lengthwise and run the leek under water, separating the center layers to clean throughout.

FRENCH ONION SOUP

SERVES 6

This classic soup gets it incredible flavor from slow-cooked, well-caramelized onions. You can roast the onions in the oven or caramelize them on top of the stove, just take your time to bring out the natural sugar and color in the onions. Use Maui or Sweet Vidalia onions in place of the basic yellow onion, for extra sweetness.

½ stick unsalted butter (for stove-top cooking only)
2 tablespoons extra-virgin olive oil
8 cups sweet yellow onions, thinly sliced
Salt and freshly ground pepper

8 cups low-sodium beef broth
½ cup Cognac or other good Brandy
6 ½-inch thick slices of French bread
2 cups Gruyere cheese, coarsely grated

TO ROAST THE ONIONS IN THE OVEN:
Preheat oven to 425°F. Toss the sliced onions with the olive oil and place in a roasting pan (do not use the butter if you are roasting the onions). Season with salt and pepper. Roast the onions, stirring every 10 minutes, for about 25 minutes or until the onions are golden. Remove the pan from the oven and add the Cognac, scraping the bottom to loosen and dissolve any caramelized bits. Transfer the onion mixture to a 3-quart pot and add the beef broth. Bring to a simmer and cook for 30 minutes.

TO CARAMELIZE THE ONIONS ON TOP OF THE STOVE:
Heat the butter and oil in a 3-quart pot over medium heat. Add the onions and season with salt and pepper. Cook slowly, stirring often, until the onions are tender and caramelized and deep caramel in color, about 30 minutes. Add the Cognac and deglaze, scraping up any browned bits from the bottom of the pan. Add the beef broth, bring to a simmer and cook for 30 minutes.

TO SERVE:
Preheat the oven to 400°F. Place the French bread slices on a baking sheet and bake in the oven until toasted, about 5 minutes. Remove the bread from the oven and top with the grated cheese. Bake until the cheese melts. Serve the cheese toasts on top of the soup.

CHEF'S TIP: To make your own Hummus, combine 1 (15-ounce) can drained chickpeas or 2 cups well cooked chickpeas, ¼ cup tahini, ¼ cup olive oil, 1 peeled garlic clove, the juice of 1 large lemon and ½ teaspoon ground cumin in your food processor. Season with salt and pepper and blend for 2 minutes or until smooth. Slowly add 1 to 2 tablespoons of water until you reach the perfect consistency.

CREAMY HUMMUS CHILI
for VEGGIE LOVERS

SERVES 4 TO 6

This recipe will delight vegetarians and even make meat-lovers swoon. The hummus adds the most wonderful texture to the chili and it's full of veggie goodness, so there's no guilt!

2 tablespoons good quality olive oil

1 small sweet yellow onion, diced

1 red bell pepper, cleaned and diced

1 green or yellow bell pepper, cleaned and diced

½ jalapeño pepper – seeds and veins removed and minced

3 garlic cloves, minced or grated

2 4-ounce cans chopped fire-roasted green chiles

1 teaspoon ground cumin

1 teaspoon dried oregano

½ teaspoon red pepper flakes

2 cups vegetable broth or water

1 15-ounce cans crushed tomatoes in juice

2 15-ounce cans white beans, drained

1 cup fresh, frozen or canned corn kernels

1 cup plain or flavored prepared hummus

Salt and freshly ground pepper

Sour cream

Green onions

Heat the olive oil in a 3-quart pot over medium heat. Add the onion and sauté until caramelized and tender, about 15 minutes, stirring often. Add the bell peppers, jalapeño, garlic and green chiles and sauté 5 minutes longer. Add the cumin, oregano and chili flakes and season with salt and pepper. Add the vegetable broth and diced tomatoes to the pot and bring the chili to a boil. Reduce the heat to low, and simmer for 20 minutes. Stir in the white beans, corn and hummus and continue cooking for 5 minutes more. Serve piping hot bowls of chili topped with dollops of sour cream and green onions.

PUMPKIN CHICKEN CHILI

SERVES 6

Pumpkin adds a wonderful creaminess and an extra layer of flavor to this easy chicken chili and is a nutrition powerhouse. This is the perfect fall food for the football season and holidays. Warm, thick, hearty, satisfying, with rich, bold flavors. Made in one pot, this comforting soup comes together in under an hour. Finish the chili with crunchy pumpkin seeds, shredded jack cheese and a squeeze of fresh lime juice.

2 tablespoons good quality olive oil	¼ teaspoon ground cinnamon
1 large sweet yellow onion, diced	1 cup pumpkin purée
1 poblano chili pepper, seeded and diced	1 28-ounce can diced tomatoes
1 red bell pepper, seeded and diced	1 tablespoon tomato paste
1 pound ground chicken	4 cups low-sodium chicken broth
2 garlic cloves, minced or grated	1 15-ounce can cannellini beans, drained and rinsed
1 tablespoon ground cumin	Salt and freshly ground pepper
1 tablespoon chili powder	Cilantro leaves, green onions and avocado
1 teaspoon sweet smoked paprika	

Heat the olive oil in a 3-quart pot over medium-high heat. Add the onions, poblano and red pepper and cook, stirring often, until tender, about 5 minutes. Increase the heat to high and add the ground chicken, garlic, cumin, chili powder, smoked paprika and cinnamon. Season the mixture with salt and pepper. Cook, stirring often, until the chicken is cooked through, about 10 minutes.

Stir in the pumpkin purée, diced tomatoes, tomato paste, chicken broth and beans. Bring the chili to a boil, reduce the heat to medium-low and cover the pot with a lid. Simmer, stirring occasionally, for 30 minutes to meld the flavors. Serve garnished with cilantro leaves, green onions and diced avocado.

SCRUMPTIOUS TURKEY CHILI

SERVES 4 TO 6

There is nothing better than a bowl of chili on a cold day! Keep it mild for the kids and add more heat with chili powder, chipotle powder or Hatch chili powder for the football crowd. Around the Thanksgiving holiday, we like to use cubed cooked turkey breast, canned pure pumpkin and brown sugar to create an entire Thanksgiving dinner in a bowl!

- 3 tablespoons good quality olive oil
- 1 small sweet yellow onion, diced
- 2 cloves garlic, minced or grated
- 1 ½ pounds ground turkey
- 2 tablespoons chili powder
- 1 teaspoon ground cumin
- 1 15-ounce can pinto beans, drained and rinsed
- 1 15-ounce can black beans, drained and rinsed
- 1 15-ounce can diced tomatoes in juice
- 2 cups low-sodium chicken broth
  Salt and freshly ground pepper
  Sour cream, shredded sharp cheddar cheese, sliced green onions, crushed corn chips or tortilla chips, avocado slices, corn kernels

Heat two tablespoons of olive oil in a 3-quart pot over medium heat. Add the onion and sauté for 5 minutes or until soft and translucent. Add the garlic and sauté for 1 minute more. Add the remaining tablespoon of oil and increase the heat to high. Add the ground turkey and cook, stirring often, breaking up the meat, until golden brown. Add the chili powder, cumin, salt and pepper. Cook for 5 minutes more, stirring often.

Add the pinto beans, black beans, diced tomatoes and the chicken broth. Cook for 10 minutes more, stirring occasionally. Adjust the seasoning.

Ladle chili into bowls and top sour cream and toppings.

THE MAIN DISH

STEAMER SMOKED SALMON

SERVES 2

Did you know that you could smoke just about anything using the steamer insert of your pot! Salmon smoked in the steamer basket, with wood chips in the pot below, creates a stovetop steamer! Chips made from alder, cherry, apple, mesquite, cedar and hickory can be used for great smoke flavor. Buy a selection of wood chips so you don't get the same smoke flavor in everything. We use alderwood chips to smoke salmon, applewood chips to smoke pork tenderloin and hickory or mesquite with meat or chicken. No soaking of chips required!

3   tablespoons alderwood chips
½   pound center cut salmon fillet, skin removed

Place the alderwood chips in the bottom of a 3-quart pot. Season the salmon with salt and pepper and place the salmon in the steamer insert. Place the steamer insert on top of the pot and cover with the lid. Cook high heat for 30 minutes; the cooking time will vary depending on the thickness of the fish. Make sure the smoke from the chips is circulating around the fish in the steamer insert. The salmon will be firm when done.

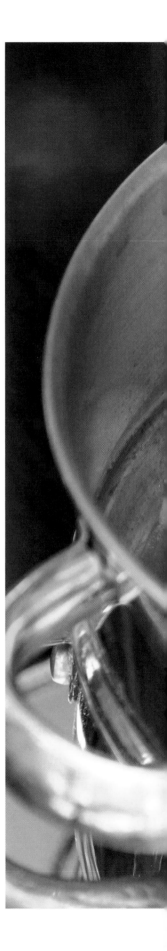

ONE POT LEMON ORZO
with SHRIMP

One pot meals are truly amazing! A super easy meal that the whole family will love. Add some asparagus at the end of cooking the orzo for something green and to give it a Spring feel and the lemon zest and juice will brighten it all. When dinnertime survival is on the line, try this fast, delicious lemon orzo pasta.

2	tablespoons good quality olive oil
1	small sweet yellow onion, diced
3	garlic cloves, minced or grated
½	teaspoon dried oregano
8	ounces orzo pasta
2 ½	cups low-sodium chicken broth
1	14.5-ounce can diced tomatoes, drained
1	bunch fresh asparagus, trimmed and cut into 1-inch pieces
	Zest and juice of 1 lemon
1	pound medium shrimp, peeled and deveined
	Salt and freshly ground pepper
¼	cup grated Parmesan cheese

Heat olive oil in a 3-quart pot over medium high heat. Add the onion and sauté, stirring often until the onion is tender and translucent, about 5 minutes. Add the garlic and oregano and cook, stirring often, for 1 minute more. Stir in the orzo and sauté until 2 minutes to toast the orzo.

Stir in the chicken broth. Bring the mixture to a boil, reduce the heat to a simmer and cover the pot. Cook for 10 minutes.

Season the shrimp with salt and pepper. Remove the lid and stir in the diced tomatoes, asparagus, lemon zest and juice and the shrimp. Replace the lid and cook on low heat for 10 minutes more, or until the shrimp are cooked through.

Finish with Parmesan cheese.

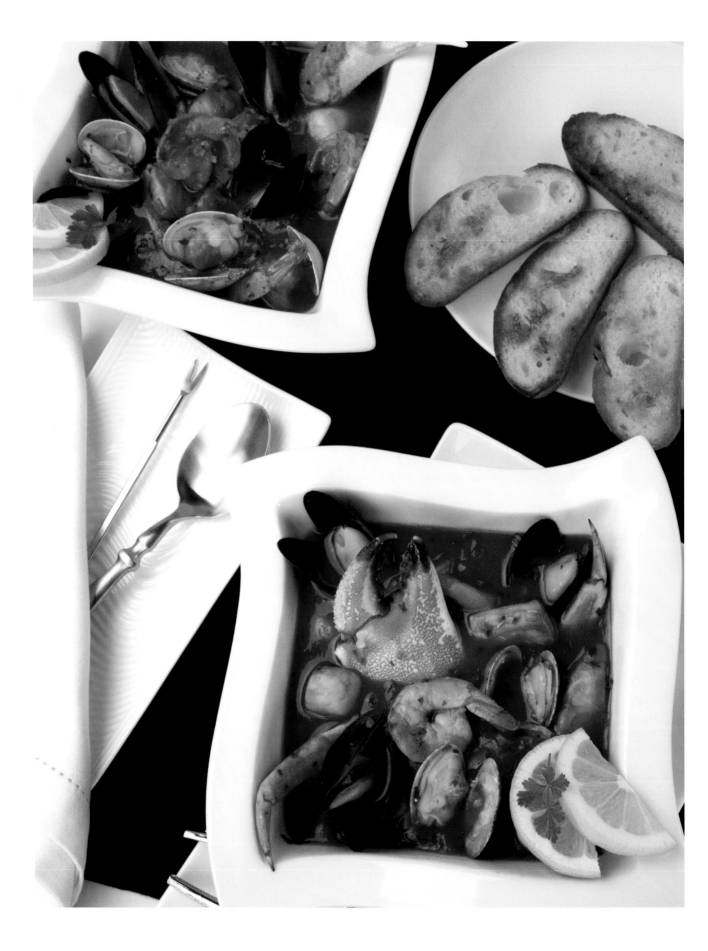

REALLY GOOD CIOPPINO

SERVES 4

This fish stew, popularized by Italian immigrants to San Francisco, is a rich tomato based broth with a wonderful seafood flavor. Use a variety of seafood in this easy and impressive crowd pleaser. This recipe is a great way to skip the oven and create a quick meal. Serve with a warm, crusty loaf of bread for mopping up the delicious sauce.

¼ cup good quality olive oil	1 28-ounce can crushed tomatoes
½ to 1 teaspoon red pepper flakes, to taste	¼ cup freshly chopped parsley
6 garlic cloves, peeled	½ pound cod or sea bass, cut into 2-inch pieces
1 bay leaf	8 large shrimp, peeled and devein
1 small sweet yellow onion, diced	8 mussels, scrubbed clean
1 celery stalk, diced	8 small clams, scrubbed clean
½ cup good quality dry white wine	Salt and freshly ground pepper
½ cup clam juice	A loaf of fresh, crusty bread – for mopping
2 cups low-sodium chicken broth	

Heat the oil over medium heat in a saucepot. Add the red pepper flakes, garlic cloves and bay leaves and cook for 2 minutes, stirring constantly.

Add the onion and celery. Sauté until the onion is tender. Add the wine and bring to a simmer. Add the clam juice, chicken broth, tomatoes, thyme, and parsley. Season with pepper. Bring to a boil, then reduce the heat to medium-low.

Season the fish with salt and pepper. Add fish to the pot and simmer 5 minutes, giving the pot a shake now and then. Do not stir your soup with a spoon after you add the fish. Add the shrimp, mussels and clams, cover the pot and cook for 8 to 10 minutes.

Remove the lid and discard any mussels or clams that do not open. Ladle the fish stew into soup bowls and garnish with a piece of toasted bread.

PINEAPPLE JALAPEÑO
SHRIMP TACOS

SERVES 4 TO 6

This six ingredient one pot dish is quick and easy to put together for a weekday dinner or Sunday supper. Delicious and healthy shrimp tacos are loaded with pineapple, jalapeños and a Lime Cilantro Crema. Add a slice of soft avocado on top and serve with rice and beans.

1 tablespoon unsalted butter

1 tablespoon good quality olive oil

2 pounds raw large shrimp, peeled and deveined

½ cup finely chopped canned or fresh pineapple

¼ cup seeded and thinly sliced jalapeños

¼ cup honey

For the Lime Cilantro Crema

1 cup sour cream

Juice of 1 lime

3 tablespoons freshly chopped cilantro

Soft corn tortillas or taco shells, shredded red cabbage, diced tomatoes, crispy bacon, crumbled Cotija cheese, fresh cilantro sprigs

Heat the butter and oil in a 3-quart pot over medium-high heat. Season the shrimp with salt and pepper and add them to the pot. Sauté the shrimp, stirring often, until they turn pink, about 3 minutes. Add the pineapple, jalapeño and honey and cook for 2 minutes more.

For the Lime Cilantro Crema, combine the ingredients in a plastic squeeze bottle or a mixing bowl and shake or whisk to blend well.

Assemble the tacos by placing shredded cabbage in the bottom of each soft tortilla or taco shell. Top with 3 cooked shrimp, drizzle the shrimp with the Lime Cilantro Crema and top with diced tomatoes, crispy bacon, crumbled cheese and a cilantro sprig.

PAN-ROASTED CLAMS

SERVES 2

Use Manila, cherry stone or littleneck clams for a great way to enjoy this quick family dinner. Enjoy with roasted baby potatoes, over spaghetti or just standing in the kitchen with a bottle of hot sauce, crusty bread and the remaining Chardonnay in the bottle! Oysters may be substituted along with slices of crisp chorizo and steamed greens.

3 tablespoons good quality olive oil
6 garlic cloves, peeled and thinly sliced
   Generous pinch of red pepper flakes
2 pounds fresh Manila (or other small) clams, scrubbed clean
   Juice of 1 lemon
1 cup of your favorite Chardonnay
2 tablespoons unsalted butter
   Salt and freshly ground pepper
   Freshly chopped parsley
   Crusty Bread, for dipping

Heat the olive oil with the garlic in a 3-quart pot over medium heat. Slowly toast the garlic slices, stirring often, until the garlic is just golden. Add the red pepper flakes to the oil and stir for 10 seconds. Add the clams and stir to coat. Squeeze in the lemon juice and add the white wine. Cover the pot with a lid and cook the clams for 5 minutes, shaking the pan often, or until all of the clams open.

Remove the lid and add a pinch of salt and freshly ground pepper to season the clams. Turn off the heat and add the butter, swirling the pan to incorporate it into the sauce. Finish with chopped parsley and serve with crusty bread.

CHINESE CASHEW CHICKEN

SERVES 4

The Chinese technique of velveting creates extra-tender chicken in just 15 minutes! Lightly coat the raw chicken with baking soda, set aside for 15 minutes, then wash off thoroughly before beginning to make the stir fry. The first time you try this, you will be amazed! The light flavored sauce and the creamy, soft crunch of cashews pairs perfectly with the extra tender chicken. Feel free to add other vegetables...Asian greens, carrots, onions and shallots. As with all stir-fries, this comes together very quickly once you start, so have everything chopped up and the sauce ready to go when you begin cooking.

---

1 pound skinless boneless chicken thighs, cut into strips
2 teaspoons baking soda
4 tablespoons soy sauce
2 tablespoons Dry Sherry
3 tablespoons oyster sauce
2 teaspoons sesame oil
1 tablespoon cornstarch
4 tablespoons water

2 tablespoons good quality olive oil
2 garlic cloves, minced or grated
½ small sweet yellow onion, sliced
1 red bell pepper, sliced
1 yellow bell pepper, sliced
¼ teaspoon dried hot red-pepper flakes
½ cup salted roasted whole cashews

Combine the baking soda and chicken in a mixing bowl, toss to coat and set aside for 15 minutes. Rinse the chicken thoroughly in a colander, then pat with paper towels and place in a clean bowl.

In another bowl, whisk together the soy sauce, Dry Sherry, oyster sauce and sesame oil. Add 3 tablespoons of the sauce mixture to the chicken and let the chicken marinate for 10 minutes. Combine the cornstarch and water in a small bowl until smooth, then add the slurry to the remaining sauce in the bowl.

Heat the olive oil over high heat in a 3-quart pot. Add the onion and cook for 2 minutes, then add the garlic and cook, stirring, for 1 minutes more. Add the chicken and bell peppers and cook until the chicken turns white on the exterior, about 2 minutes. Add the sauce to the pot, bring to a simmer and cook for 3 to 4 minutes or until the sauce thickens and the chicken is cooked through. Stir in the cashews and serve with rice.

GINGER CHICKEN

SERVES 4

An easy-on-the-budget chicken dish with Asian flavors which will become a family favorite. Serve with soba noodles or make coconut rice using coconut milk. Marinate for an hour or for more flavor up to 24 hours.

6 tablespoons soy sauce
3 tablespoons honey
2 tablespoons seasoned rice wine vinegar
2 tablespoons freshly grated ginger
2 teaspoons sesame oil
4 boneless, skinless chicken breasts, cut into ½-inch strips
8 ounces soba noodles or whole-wheat spaghetti, cooked and drained
¼ cup fresh cilantro leaves
¼ cup fresh mint leaves
Toasted sesame seeds

Combine the soy sauce, honey, vinegar, ginger and sesame oil in a resealable plastic bag and shake to combine. Add the chicken breast strips and marinate the chicken in the refrigerator for at least an hour.

Heat the sesame oil in a 3-quart pot. Cook the chicken, stirring occasionally, until it is golden brown and cooked through, about 8 minutes. Add the cooked noodles, cilantro leaves and mint leaves and toss to combine. Finish with toasted sesame seeds.

WEEKDAY CHICKEN PARMESAN PASTA BAKE

SERVES 4

Healthier than frying and very kid friendly. We love anything chicken parm; subs, pizza and especially this parm pasta bake. It's a complete meal that feels like it took hours to make! For extra speedy prep, use frozen breaded chicken breasts. Use thin chicken breast slices and Fontina or provolone instead of mozzarella for a lighter dish.

- 1 pound frozen breaded chicken breasts
- 3 tablespoons good quality olive oil
- 4 cloves garlic, thinly sliced
- 2 cups marinara sauce
- ¾ pound penne pasta, cooked and drained
- 2 cups shredded mozzarella cheese
- ¼ cup grated Parmesan cheese
- Salt and freshly ground pepper
- Small handful fresh basil leaves, cut into thin strips

Microwave the chicken according to package directions. When cool enough to handle, cut into large chunks.

Heat the olive oil in a 3-quart pot over medium heat. Add the sliced garlic and cook for 1 minute. Add the chicken and cook, stirring often, until crispy and golden-brown, about 2 minutes. Transfer the chicken and garlic to a plate.

Add the marinara sauce and the cooked pasta to the pot along with half of the mozzarella cheese. Stir until the pasta is coated with the sauce and the cheese has melted. Stir in the reserved chicken. Top of the pasta with the remaining mozzarella cheese and sprinkle the top with Parmesan cheese.

Preheat your broiler to high heat. Place the pot under the broiler until the cheese has melted. Finish with fresh basil.

CHICKEN CURRY
with COCONUT JASMINE RICE

SERVES 4 TO 6

There is loads of personality in this one-pot, relatively quick, ideal all-purpose meal. Using a rotisserie chicken cuts your prep time in half. If your family or guests like the fiery factor, add more chilies and spices to take the dish a few notches higher.

1 tablespoon good quality olive oil	3 tablespoons freshly squeezed lime juice
1 small red onion, sliced	2 tablespoons packed dark brown sugar
1 to 2 tablespoons Thai red curry paste	3 cups shredded rotisserie chicken
1 14-ounce can unsweetened coconut milk	1 14 ½-ounce can diced tomatoes in juice - drained
1 cup low-sodium chicken broth or water	1 cup basil leaves, torn

Place the oil in a 3-quart casserole over medium heat. Add the onion and cook until soft, about 5 minutes. Stir in the curry paste and cook for 2 minutes more. Stir in the coconut milk, chicken broth, lime juice and brown sugar and bring to a boil. Add the shredded chicken and the diced tomatoes to the pot and bring to a simmer. Cover and cook for 10 minutes. Add salt and pepper to taste. Finish with basil and serve with Coconut Jasmine Rice.

COCONUT JASMINE RICE MAKES 4 CUPS

2 tablespoons canola oil	1 14-ounce can unsweetened coconut milk
1 ½ cups jasmine rice	2 teaspoons granulated sugar
2 cups water	Pinch of salt

For the rice, heat the canola oil in a small pot with a lid. Add the rice and sauté, stirring often, until the rice is fragrant, about 2 minutes. Add the water, coconut milk, sugar and salt. Bring the mixture to a boil, reduce the heat to simmer and cover the pot. Simmer for 15 to 18 minutes, or until the liquid has been absorbed by the rice. When the rice is done, turn off the heat, remove the lid and cover the top of the pot with a kitchen towel, then replace the lid and allow the rice to stand for 5 minutes more.

CLASSIC CHICKEN POT PIE

SERVES 4

An all-time Autumn favorite in our family, using shredded rotisserie chicken (or leftover turkey) and store-bought puff pastry.

6 tablespoons unsalted butter
1 tablespoon good quality olive oil
½ small sweet yellow onion, diced
2 large carrots, peeled and sliced ¼-inch thick
1 stalk celery, sliced ¼-inch thick
4 tablespoons all-purpose flour
1 teaspoon freshly chopped thyme
2 cups low-sodium chicken broth
1 cup half & half
2 cups store-bought rotisserie chicken, shredded

1 cup frozen petite peas
1 tablespoon freshly chopped parsley
Flaked sea salt and freshly ground pepper

For the Crust:

1 whole egg
1 teaspoon water
1 sheet frozen puff pastry, thawed and chilled

Preheat the oven to 375°F.

Melt 2 tablespoons of butter along with the olive oil in 3-quart pot over medium heat. Add the onions and sauté until translucent, about 10 minutes. Add the carrots and celery and season the mixture with salt and pepper. Sauté 5 minutes more, stirring often. Add the cooked chicken, potato, peas and parsley. Adjust the seasoning and cook 5 minutes more, stirring often.

In a separate 3-quart pot, melt the remaining 4 tablespoons of butter. Stir in the flour and cook the roux for 6 to 8 minutes, stirring constantly. Add the chicken broth and half & half and bring to a boil, whisking often. Reduce the heat to a simmer and cook for 10 minutes or until the sauce thickens. Add the sautéed vegetable mixture to the sauce and stir to combine. Remove the pot from the heat and allow the mixture to cool slightly.

Whisk the egg and water together in a small bowl. Place the cold puff pastry sheet on a floured work surface and cut an 8x8-inch square. Lay on the top of the pot, so that the egg wash helps the sides of the pastry adhere to the exterior of the pot. Brush the top of the puff pastry with egg wash. Bake for 25-30 minutes or until puffed and golden.

LEFTOVER TURKEY COBBLER
with BUTTERMILK BISCUITS

SERVES 4 TO 6

We top this thick, chunky, very flavorful stew with buttermilk biscuits or a buttery pastry crust. Mashed potatoes or roasted sweet potatoes work well too. We usually have lots of leftovers of juicy turkey meat, gravy, caramelized carrots and parsnips and herb stuffing with mushrooms and onions. Use the amounts listed as a guide for your own leftovers and use chicken or turkey stock to adjust the consistency of the stew. Thanksgiving leftovers never tasted so good!

2	cups leftover gravy
1 to 1½	cups leftover stuffing
2	cups leftover assorted cooked vegetables, cut into 1-inch pieces
3	cups leftover turkey, shredded
½	cup apple cider
	Turkey stock or low-sodium chicken broth
¼	cup chopped fresh Italian parsley
	Salt and freshly ground pepper
4	store-bought or homemade buttermilk biscuits

Combine the gravy and stuffing in a 3-quart pot and stir until combined. Place the pot over medium heat and bring to a boil, stirring often. Reduce the heat and simmer gently until the stuffing dissolves. Add the vegetables and turkey, season the mixture with salt and pepper, and stir until blended. Add the apple cider and simmer until heated through. If the mixture is too thick, add turkey stock, a little at a time, until the mixture resembles a stew.

Simmer until piping hot. Just before serving, stir in the chopped parsley. Split the biscuits in half. Ladle the stew into bowls and top with a half of a buttermilk biscuit.

SESAME BEEF STIR FRY

SERVES 4

The Holy Trinity of Cantonese cooking...garlic, ginger, soy...provides the perfect base for any good stir fry. Spice this up using some gochujang, a Korean red chile paste, or use your favorite Cantonese hot chili oil. Serve with garlic fried rice.

- 2   tablespoons low-sodium beef broth
- 2   tablespoons low-sodium soy sauce
- 1   teaspoon honey
-     Pinch of red pepper flakes
- 1   pound flank steak or boneless top sirloin steak, cut into thin strips
- 1   tablespoon cornstarch
- 2   teaspoons five-spice powder
- 2   tablespoons good quality olive oil
- 1   tablespoon dark sesame oil
- 3   garlic cloves, minced or grated
- 1   tablespoon freshly grated ginger
- 1   cup sliced yellow bell pepper
- 2   cups snow peas
- ¼   cup toasted sesame seeds

In a small mixing bowl, combine the beef broth, soy sauce, honey and red pepper flakes. Set aside.

Combine the cornstarch and five-spice powder in a plastic bag and add the slices of steak. Toss to coat the meat well. Heat the olive oil in a 3-quart pot over high heat until the oil is almost smoking. Add the steak and cook, stirring, until golden all over. Transfer the meat to a plate and add the sesame oil to the same pot. Add the garlic, ginger, bell pepper and snow peas and sauté for 2 minutes. Add the meat back to the pot long with the beef broth mixture and cook for 3 minutes, or until the meat is heated through and the sauce has reduced to a glaze. Finish with toasted sesame seeds.

MOZZARELLA STUFFED MEATBALL HOAGIES

SERVES 6

These deliciously flavored meatballs served on hoagie rolls will be your new favorite at your weeknight dinner or next football party. The ultimate hoagie meatball with a mozzarella ball inside!

- ¼ cup dry breadcrumbs
- ½ cup whole milk
- 1 pound lean ground beef
- 1 tablespoon good quality olive oil
- 2 garlic cloves, minced or grated
- 2 tablespoons freshly chopped parsley
- ½ cup grated Parmesan cheese, plus more for serving
- 1 large egg
- 24 bocconcini (mini balls of fresh mozzarella cheese)
- 4 cups homemade or store-bought marinara sauce
- 6 Hoagie rolls, buttered and toasted
  Salt and freshly ground pepper

In a medium bowl, soak the breadcrumbs in the milk. Add the ground beef, olive oil, chopped garlic, parsley, Parmesan cheese, the egg along with 1 teaspoon of salt and ½ teaspoon of pepper to the soaked breadcrumbs and stir to combine. Place about 2 tablespoons of the mixture in your hand and press a fresh mozzarella ball into the center. Shape the meat around the cheese, forming a meatball. Repeat with the remaining meat and mozzarella.

Bring the marinara sauce to a simmer over in a 3-quart pot over medium heat. Add the meatballs and cook gently, until the meatballs are cooked through, about 30 minutes.

Cook the meatballs in the tomato sauce until cooked through. Spoon the meatballs with the sauce into the toasted hoagie rolls.

ONE-POT FUSILLI
and MEATBALLS

SERVES 4 TO 6

Break the tradition and use fusilli for a fun twist! Hearty, healthy and everyone's favorite dish. A new kitchen trick is to use chicken broth instead of water to cook the fusilli and <u>do not drain the pasta</u>! There should be about a tablespoon or two of liquid left when the noodles reach the desired consistency – the broth will add depth to the sauce.

---

2 tablespoons unsalted butter or bacon fat
2 garlic cloves, minced or grated
3 cups low-sodium chicken broth
½ pound fusilli bucati (long fusilli) or regular fusilli
2 cups marinara sauce
1 ½ cups shredded mozzarella cheese
¾ pound frozen pre-cooked Italian style meatballs, thawed
½ cup grated Parmesan cheese
   Salt and freshly ground pepper
   Freshly chopped basil

Preheat the oven to 350°F. Melt the butter in a 3-quart pot over medium heat. Add the garlic and sauté for 2 minutes, stirring often.

Add the broth and bring to a boil over high heat. Add the pasta and cook according to package directions, stirring frequently, except DO NOT DRAIN the pasta.

Remove the pot from the heat. Stir 1 cup of the marinara sauce into the pasta, season with salt and pepper and mix well. Top with the shredded mozzarella cheese. Place the thawed meatballs evenly over the cheese. Spoon the remaining marinara sauce over the meatballs and sprinkle with the Parmesan cheese.

Transfer the pot to the oven and bake for 20 minutes or until heated through. Finish with basil.

BRATS + KIMCHI

SERVES 6

Korean Kimchi is a spicy, funky Korean cabbage that is bottled and sold in most markets. It is a very fiery, salty, tart, flavorful condiment that can be mixed into fried rice, soups, omelets, as a taco topping and to top a hot dog. Crumbled bacon will finish this hoagie roll perfectly and please your football crowd! Serve with tender-in-the-center, crisp-on-the-outside fried tator tots!

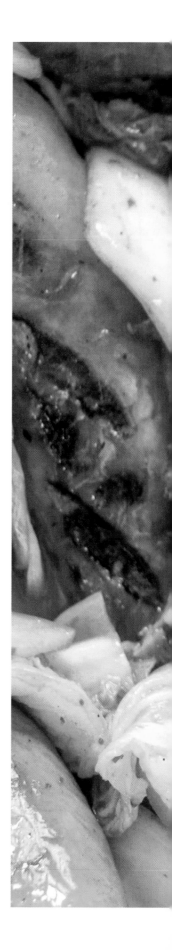

1	tablespoon unsalted butter
1	tablespoon good quality olive oil
1	small sweet yellow onion, thinly sliced
2	green apples – halved, cored and thinly sliced
6	bratwurst
1	tablespoon honey
2	cups low-sodium chicken broth
1	14-ounce jar Kimchi

Combine the butter and oil in a 3-quart pot over medium heat. Add the onions and sauté, stirring often, for 5 minutes. Add the apples and sauté for 5 minutes more.

Meanwhile, preheat the oven to broil. Place the brats on a baking sheet and broil for 5 minutes, turning once, until golden brown.

Add the brats, honey, chicken broth and Kimchi to the onions and apples and bring to a boil. Reduce the heat to a simmer and cook for 30 minutes.

Serve on hoagie rolls with stone ground brown mustard.

ON
THE
SIDE

SOURDOUGH APPLE STUFFING

SERVES 6

The American Holiday Table is all the better with a beautiful bird and a savory stuffing/dressing. Stuffing is by far our favorite of the Thanksgiving leftovers. Add mushrooms, use Challah or cornbread, dried fruit, even oysters, to modify any of our stuffing/dressing recipes.

---

2 ½   pounds sourdough bread, crust trimmed and cut into ½-inch cubes

½   pound thick-cut bacon, cut into ½-inch pieces

2   medium sweet yellow onions, diced

3   celery stalks, diced

2   Gala or Fuji apples – peeled, cored and diced

1   cup pecan halves, toasted

¼   cup freshly chopped parsley

1   tablespoon fresh sage, chopped

3   large eggs, beaten

8   tablespoons (1 stick) unsalted butter, melted

2   cups low-sodium chicken broth

Salt and freshly ground pepper

Preheat the oven to 350°F. Spread the bread cubes in a single layer onto two baking sheets. Bake until lightly toasted, about 12 minutes, tossing once during baking. Remove from the oven and let cool. Transfer to a large mixing bowl.

Cook the diced bacon until crisp. Add the onions and celery and sauté until tender, about 5 minutes. Add the apples and sauté 3 minutes more.

Add the bacon mixture to the bread cubes along with the nuts, parsley and sage and mix well. Add the eggs and melted butter and mix to combine. Add enough stock to moisten the mixture. Season with salt and pepper. Spoon the mixture into a buttered 3-quart casserole. Cover and bake at 350°F for 45 minutes. Uncover and bake 15 minutes more, or until the top is golden and crisp.

OUR KITCHEN NOTES: All of our stuffing recipes, without the broth/stock and eggs, can be assembled, but not baked, one day ahead and refrigerated, covered. Just before baking, stir in the chicken broth and eggs.

HOLIDAY SWEET SAVORY STUFFING

SERVES 6

A new stuffing recipe with the wonderful flavors of pancetta, fennel, pears and dried cranberries changes the classic stuffing/dressing into crazy delicious, with notes of sweet and savory. It has great flavor and it's very simple to make.

---

1 22-ounce day-old Italian, Ciabatta or Country Bread, cut into ¾-inch cubes
2 tablespoons good quality olive oil
1 large fennel bulb, trimmed and diced
4 ounces pancetta, cut into ¼-inch dice (bacon works great, too)
1 small sweet yellow onion, diced
3 garlic cloves, minced or grated
2 large Anjou or Bartlett pears, chopped

1 cup dried cranberries
3 cups turkey stock or low-sodium chicken broth
¼ cup freshly chopped parsley
1 tablespoon finely chopped fresh rosemary
1 tablespoon finely chopped fresh sage leaves
8 tablespoons (1 stick) unsalted butter, melted
2 large eggs, beaten
Salt and freshly ground pepper

Preheat the oven to 350°F. Spread the bread cubes in a single layer onto two baking sheets. Bake until lightly toasted, about 12 minutes, tossing once during baking. Remove from the oven and let cool. Transfer to a large mixing bowl.

Heat the olive oil in a 3-quart pot over medium heat. Add the pancetta and cook for 5 minutes or until crisp, then remove with a slotted spoon and drain on paper towels.

In the same pot, add the fennel and onion. Cook for 10 minutes, stirring often, or until the vegetables are tender and golden. Add the garlic, pears and cranberries and cook for 3 minutes, stirring occasionally. Add the broth, bring the mixture to a boil, then reduce the heat and simmer for 5 minutes.

Add the vegetable mixture to the bread cubes. Stir in the crisped pancetta, parsley, rosemary, sage and melted butter and season liberally with salt and pepper. Add the eggs and mix well.

Butter a 3-quart pot. Spoon the stuffing into the pot and cover with a lid or aluminum foil. Bake for 30 minutes, then uncover and bake 20 minutes more or until golden brown on top.

OUR KITCHEN NOTES: Stuffing/dressing can be baked 6 hours ahead and cooled completely, uncovered, then refrigerated, loosely covered. Reheat, covered, in a 400°F oven until hot, about 20 to 30 minutes.

GINGER SPICED CRANBERRY CHUTNEY

MAKES ABOUT 3 CUPS

This year, buy a couple of bags of fresh cranberries, and make the homemade stuff! This chutney is a little more complex and sweet, spicy and delicious. You can make it well in advance by putting it into tightly sealed canning jars in the refrigerator just waiting for the big day. Be sure to set aside a jar for the turkey sandwiches! Also, it's so good with a cheddar or cave-aged blue drizzled with honey.

2 12-ounce bags fresh cranberries
2 large ripe pears – peeled, cored and diced
1 cup packed dark brown sugar
1 cup granulated sugar
2 teaspoons ground ginger
1 teaspoon pure vanilla extract
  Zest and juice of 1 lemon
1 cinnamon stick
  Pinch of salt

Combine all of the ingredients in a 3-quart pot. Bring to a boil over medium heat, stirring constantly. Reduce the heat to low and continue cooking, stirring often, until the mixture thickens and the cranberries burst, about 15 minutes. Add a pinch of salt and cool completely. Remove the cinnamon stick before serving.

SOUTHERN STYLE CORNBREAD DRESSING with SAUSAGE and SAGE

SERVES 6

A southern Thanksgiving classic that we have on our holiday table every year. If you've never made it before, keep an eye on the amount of broth you put in; you want it to be the consistency of cornbread mix, don't let it get soupy. Sometimes you need more broth and sometimes you need less! Some nice additions are diced red pepper, corn or creamed corn.

8 cups (about 2 pounds) store-bought or homemade cornbread, crumbled into small pieces
8 tablespoons (1 stick) unsalted butter
1 pound sweet Italian sausage, squeezed from the casing
1 large sweet yellow onion, diced
3 stalks celery, diced
2 garlic cloves, minced or grated
¼ cup freshly chopped sage leaves
4 large eggs, beaten
3 to 4 cups low-sodium chicken broth
¼ cup freshly chopped parsley
Salt and freshly ground pepper

Preheat the oven to 375°F. Butter a 3-quart casserole.

Spread the crumbled cornbread in a single layer onto a baking sheet. Bake until lightly toasted, about 12 minutes, tossing once during baking. Remove from the oven and let cool.

Melt the butter in a 3-quart pot over medium-high heat. Add the sausage and cook, breaking up the meat, until golden, about 8 minutes. Add the onion, celery, garlic and sage and cook, stirring often, until vegetables are tender, about 15 minutes.

Place the toasted cornbread in a large mixing bowl and add the sausage mixture. Add the eggs and 2 ½ cups of the broth and fold gently until evenly mixed. Add more broth as needed. Season liberally with salt and pepper and stir in the parsley.

Transfer the dressing to the prepared saucepot. Place a lid on the pot and bake the dressing for 30 minutes. Remove the lid and continue baking for 30 minutes more, or until the dressing is golden brown and crisped on top.

SWEET POTATO CASSEROLE
with PRALINE TOPPING

SERVES 8

This glorious mash gets packed into a buttered 3-quart pot and praline topped. Make the casserole ahead, cover and refrigerate for up to 2 days. The leftover sweet potatoes can be folded into a pancake batter with a hint of nutmeg!

3 pounds sweet potatoes, peeled and cubed
1 cup all-purpose flour
¾ cup packed dark brown sugar
½ cup pecans, chopped and toasted
2 tablespoons unsalted butter, melted
½ teaspoon ground cinnamon
½ cup heavy whipping cream
2 teaspoons freshly grated orange zest
¼ teaspoon ground ginger
Salt and freshly ground pepper

Cook the sweet potatoes in a large pot of boiling salted water until tender, about 30 minutes. Drain well.

Preheat the oven to 350°F.

For the topping, combine the flour, ¼ cup of the brown sugar, pecans, butter and cinnamon in a small mixing bowl. Set aside.

Place the cooked sweet potatoes in a large mixing bowl with the cream, orange peel, ground ginger and the remaining ¼ cup brown sugar. Mash the mixture together until smooth. Season to taste with salt and pepper.

Butter a 3-quart pot. Transfer the sweet potato mixture to a 3-quart pot. Cover the surface of the sweet potatoes with the topping mixture.

Bake the casserole for 30 minutes, or until the topping is golden and the casserole is heated through.

LOADED MASHED POTATO CASSEROLE

SERVES 6

Mashed potatoes are no longer boring. Easy and delicious, and a new family favorite. This is fun to make and simple enough for the kids to help. If you have leftovers, add some milk or cream, reheat, and you've got a loaded potato soup!

2 heads garlic
5 pounds russet potatoes, peeled and cut into quarters
8 tablespoons (1 stick) unsalted butter
4 ounces cream cheese
1 cup sour cream
½ cup whole milk, if needed
2 cups shredded white cheddar cheese
8 slices thick-cut bacon, cooked and crumbled
Chopped chives

Preheat the oven to 350°F. Cut the top third off of each garlic bulb, drizzle with olive oil and season with salt and pepper. Wrap tightly in aluminum foil and roast for 1 hour or until the garlic cloves are caramelized and tender. Squeeze the roasted garlic cloves from the head of garlic and set aside.

In a 3-quart pot, cook the potatoes in salted water for 15 minutes or until very tender. Drain the potatoes and return them to the pot. Add the butter and mash the potatoes using a potato masher. Add the roasted garlic, cream cheese and sour cream and mix to combine. If the mixture is too thick, add milk to thin. Add the cheddar cheese and crumbled bacon into the potato mixture and stir. Season the potatoes with salt and pepper. Finish with chopped chives.

HERB + PARMESAN
MONKEY BREAD

SERVES 8

It's easy to become hooked on this tender pull-apart loaf, hot from the oven. Watch it disappear when served alongside a steaming bowl of soup or with a main course to sop up any sauce left on your plate. Baking bread has never been so easy or so delicious.

8   tablespoons (1 stick) unsalted butter
2   garlic cloves, minced or grated
2   cups grated Parmesan cheese
3   tablespoons freshly chopped rosemary
3   tablespoons freshly chopped thyme
3   tablespoons freshly chopped parsley
    Freshly ground pepper
3   7.5-ounce tubes refrigerated buttermilk biscuits

Preheat the oven to 350°F. Butter a 3-quart casserole.

Combine the butter and garlic in a microwave-safe shallow bowl and microwave until the butter is completely melted. In another shallow mixing bowl combine the Parmesan cheese with the fresh herbs and pepper.

Cut the thawed dough into 24 equal pieces and gently roll each piece of dough into a ball. Drop a few balls of dough at a time into the melted butter and coat well. Drop each dough ball into the cheese mixture and toss to coat. Place the coated balls in the prepared pan, about ½-inch apart, staggering the balls to create the pull-apart effect after baking. Continue the process with the remaining balls of dough.

Bake for 20 to 25 minutes or until golden brown (the top of the bread should sound hollow when tapped). Remove the monkey bread from the oven and cool slightly before inverting onto a plate.

PARSNIP and CAULIFLOWER PURÉE
with ROASTED GARLIC

SERVES 6 TO 8

Sweet parsnips and cauliflower combine to create a surprisingly easy, comforting side dish. It's a healthy alternative (no butter or cream!) to mashed potatoes and the purée can be made ahead; just cool and refrigerate until ready to serve. Rewarm over low heat.

---

2 tablespoons good quality olive oil
2 pounds cauliflower florets
½ pound parsnips, peeled and cut into 1-inch rounds
1 head of roasted garlic, cloves squeezed from the bulb
Salt and freshly ground white pepper
1 ½ cups whole milk

Heat the olive oil in a 3-quart pot over medium-high heat and add the cauliflower and parsnips. Season with salt and pepper and sauté over medium heat for 5 minutes, stirring often.

Add the milk and bring to a boil, then reduce to a simmer. Cook until the vegetables are knife tender, about 20 minutes.

Transfer the mixture, including the liquid, to the bowl of a food processor. Add the roasted garlic and blend until smooth. Season with salt and pepper, to taste. Return the purée to the pot and serve hot.

ROASTED CAULIFOWER GRATIN
with GOAT CHEESE

SERVES 6

The best way to cook cauliflower is definitely roasting. Roasting produces an unbelievably sweet and nutty flavor and gives it a texture that's both crispy and tender. The goat cheese adds a tart, tangy bite and the creamy sauce adds character. We love this side dish with pork or chicken or on a holiday buffet.

2 tablespoons good quality olive oil

1 large head of cauliflower, trimmed and cut into small florets

1 cup fresh breadcrumbs

4 tablespoons unsalted butter

1 small sweet yellow onion, diced

2 garlic cloves, minced or grated

1 teaspoon fresh thyme leaves

2 tablespoons all-purpose flour

1 ½ cups whole milk

4 ounces soft goat cheese

Flaked sea salt & white pepper

Freshly chopped chives

Preheat the oven to 400°F. Place the cauliflower florets on a baking sheet and drizzle with 1 tablespoon of oil. Season with salt and pepper and toss to coat. Roast the cauliflower for 15 minutes.

Meanwhile, melt 1 tablespoon of butter in a small sauté pan. Add the breadcrumbs, season with salt and pepper and toast for 3 minutes until lightly browned.

Heat 1 tablespoon of butter with the olive oil over medium heat in a 3-quart pot. Add the onions and sauté, stirring often, until tender and beginning to caramelize, about 10 minutes. Add the garlic and thyme and sauté 1 minute more. Add the remaining 2 tablespoons of butter to the pot to melt. Add the flour and stir to combine. Cook for 2 minutes, stirring often. Slowly add the milk and whisk constantly until the sauce thickens, about 5 minutes. Stir in the goat cheese. Add the roasted cauliflower and toss to coat. Taste and season with salt and pepper.

Bake for 20 minutes, until the top is beginning to brown in spots. Remove from oven and sprinkle the top with the toasted breadcrumbs. Bake for 5 minutes more.

CHEF'S TIP: To roast garlic, use whole heads of garlic in their skin or peeled garlic cloves. If using a head of garlic, cut the bulb in half and drizzle with olive oil. Wrap tightly in aluminum foil and roast at 375°F for 1 hour or until the garlic cloves are soft. For individually peeled garlic cloves, drizzle a handful of cloves with olive oil and season with salt and pepper. Wrap the seasoned cloves in aluminum foil and roast for 30 minutes. Allow the garlic to cool and squeeze the pulp out of the skins or puree the peeled cloves.

GREEN BEANS
with SMOKED BACON

SERVES 6

This flavorful side dish is a Thanksgiving staple and becomes a year round dish with a smoky, slightly sweet bacon vinaigrette. A simple, fast way to bring bacon and green beans to the table.

- 1 pounds applewood green beans, stems removed
- 1 tablespoon good quality olive oil
- ½ pound thick-cut bacon, cut into ½-inch pieces
- 1 small sweet yellow onion, thinly sliced
- ⅓ cup red wine vinegar
- 1 tablespoon granulated sugar
- ¼ cup freshly chopped parsley
  Freshly ground pepper

Boil or steam the green beans for 3 minutes or until crisp tender. Remove the beans and place them in an ice bath to cool.

Heat the olive oil in a 3-quart pot with the bacon and cook, stirring often, until it begins to brown. Add the onion and cook until the bacon and onion are caramelized and golden, stirring, about 10 minutes more.

Drain the green beans from the ice water and pat dry. Add the green beans, vinegar and sugar to the bacon and onions and cook until the sugar has dissolved. Mix in the parsley and season with pepper. Cook for 2 minutes more or until heated through.

PASTA
+
RICE

CJG'S MAC N' CHEESE

SERVES 6

This recipe is easily doubled – because one can't have too much mac n' cheese! An essential recipe to add to your top five. The crunchy stuff on top can be replaced with jalapeños and crumbled bacon. Easy, extra-creamy, classic, comforting...

---

1   pound macaroni or other curly noodle

For the Topping

½   cup Japanese bread crumbs (Panko)
½   cup grated Parmesan cheese
3   tablespoons unsalted butter, melted

For the Filling

5   tablespoons unsalted butter
3   tablespoons all-purpose flour
3   cups whole milk
1   cup shredded white cheddar cheese
1   cup shredded Fontina cheese
½   cup shredded Gruyere cheese
¼   cup ricotta cheese
2   tablespoons crumbled blue cheese
Salt and freshly ground pepper

Cook the pasta shells in salted boiling water until al dente. Drain well.

In a saucepot over medium heat, melt the butter. Add the flour and cook, stirring often for 2 minutes, to create a roux. Slowly add the milk, whisking constantly, and bring the mixture to a simmer. The Béchamel Sauce will thicken as it cooks. Reduce the heat and add the white cheddar cheese, Fontina, Gruyere and ricotta. Stir slowly until all the cheeses melt completely. Add the blue cheese and cooked pasta and stir until combined. Season to taste with salt and pepper.

Melt the butter in a small sauté pan and add the Panko crumbs. Cook over medium heat, stirring often, until the Panko crumbs are golden. Remove from the heat and stir in the Parmesan cheese.

Serve the Mac n' Cheese in bowls with a spoonful of the toasted bread crumbs on top.

CHEESY BAKED RIGATONI
with PANCETTA

SERVES 6

The four cheeses tossed with cooked rigatoni and pancetta, ham or spicy sausage is warm and filling. The easy cheesy sauce (a white sauce, also called Béchamel sauce without the cheese) is the perfect base for mac and cheese, Alfredo pasta or white country gravy). It goes perfectly with Focaccia bread and a bottle of Chianti.

---

3 tablespoons unsalted butter	1 cup shredded mozzarella cheese
¼ cup dry breadcrumbs	1 cup shredded provolone cheese
¼ cup grated Parmesan cheese	1 cup shredded Fontina cheese
1 tablespoon good quality olive oil	¾ pound rigatoni pasta, cooked and drained
6 ounces pancetta, diced	Salt and freshly ground pepper
3 tablespoons all-purpose flour	
3 cups whole milk	

Preheat the oven to 375°F.

Melt 1 tablespoon of butter in a small sauté pan over low heat. Add the breadcrumbs and toss well. Set aside to cool, then mix in the Parmesan cheese.

Heat the olive oil in a 3-quart pot over medium heat. Add the pancetta and sauté until crisp and golden, about 8 minutes. Add the remaining 2 tablespoons of butter to the pot. Add the flour and cook for 2 minutes, stirring constantly. Gradually add the milk and cook over medium heat, whisking often, until the mixture is thick and bubbly, about 5 minutes. Add the mozzarella, provolone and Fontina cheese and stir until the cheeses melt. Season the cheese sauce with salt and pepper, to taste.

Add the cooked pasta to the cheese sauce and stir to combine. Cover and bake for 20 minutes or until bubbly. Uncover the pasta and sprinkle the top with the breadcrumb mixture. Bake 10 minutes more or until golden brown.

PENNE PUTTANESCA

SERVES 4

A fabulous vegetarian dish (take out the anchovies!) and a great Sunday supper. Keep all of the ingredients in your pantry for a quick dinner and use spaghetti, linguine or vermicelli for a delicious change-up.

⅓ cup good quality olive oil
5 garlic cloves, minced or grated
2 teaspoons anchovy paste
½ teaspoon red pepper flakes
1 28-ounce can diced tomatoes
1 tablespoon tomato paste
½ cup pitted Kalamata olives
2 tablespoons drained capers
   Pinch of granulated sugar
½ cup coarsely chopped fresh basil
¾ pound penne pasta, cooked and drained
   Salt and freshly ground pepper
   Grated Parmesan cheese

Heat the olive oil in a 3-quart pot over medium heat. Add the garlic and sauté until tender and lightly golden, about 2 minutes, stirring often. Add the anchovy fillets and stir to dissolve. Increase the heat and add the red pepper flakes, diced tomatoes, tomato paste, olives, capers, sugar and basil. Season with salt and pepper and simmer for 10 minutes to blend the flavors.

Add the cooked pasta and toss to combine. Finish with Parmesan cheese.

SPAGHETTI CARBONARA

SERVES 4

Six ingredients that come together in under 30 minutes! One of our all-time favorite classic Italian pasta dishes. This is creamy comfort food with a luxurious sauce worthy of a special occasion. Serve it with a crisp Caesar salad, a loaf of ciabatta and a bottle of red wine.

½   pound applewood-smoked bacon, cut into 1-inch pieces
1   small sweet yellow onion, finely chopped
¼   cup dry white wine
¾   pound spaghetti, cooked and drained
3   large eggs
1   cup grated Parmesan cheese
    Freshly ground black pepper

Cook the bacon in 3-quart casserole over moderate heat, stirring, until the fat begins to render, about 3 minutes. Add the onion and cook, stirring occasionally, until the onion is golden and the bacon is cooked but not crisp, about 10 minutes. Add the white wine and simmer until reduced by half, about 2 minutes.

Whisk together the eggs and Parmesan cheese in a mixing bowl. Add the cooked spaghetti to the bacon mixture and toss to coat. Remove the pot from the heat and add the egg mixture, stirring to combine. Place the pot over low heat and cook for 1 minute. Season with pepper and serve immediately.

PENNE with ROASTED BUTTERNUT SQUASH and BROWN BUTTER

SERVES 6

We created this recipe with thoughts of the bright orange pasta that comes out of a box, but much fancier! A silky sauce made from Roasted Butternut squash and brown butter. Garnish with more fried sage leaves and Parmesan.

---

2   tablespoons good quality olive oil
1   12-ounce bag cleaned and cubed butternut squash
2   shallots, peeled and quartered
¼   cup dry white wine
8   tablespoons (1 stick) unsalted butter
12 fresh sage leaves
½   cup chopped walnuts, toasted
1   pound penne pasta, cooked and drained
½   cup grated Parmesan cheese
    Salt and freshly ground pepper

Preheat the oven to 425°F. Spread the butternut squash cubes and the shallots on a baking sheet in a single layer. Drizzle with 2 tablespoons of olive oil and season with salt and pepper. Roast for 20 minutes, or until the squash is cooked through and caramelized. Remove the baking sheet from the oven and pour the white wine over the vegetables. Bake for 5 minutes longer.

Transfer the roasted squash and shallots, with any liquid left on the baking sheet, to a food processor and process until smooth.

Melt the butter in a 3-quart pot over medium heat. Cook over medium heat until the butter is amber in color and has a nutty aroma. Add the sage leaves and walnuts and cook for 1 minute, stirring constantly. Stir in the roasted butternut squash and mix well. Add the drained pasta and ¼ cup of the Parmesan cheese. Finish the pasta with the remaining Parmesan cheese.

SPRINGTIME VEGETARIAN PASTA

SERVES 4

One of our favorite things to do on Spring weekends is to go to the farmer's market. We love local food...the fresher the better. Whether it's springtime or just when the weather is beginning to cool, the bunches of vegetables in your fridge will create a big, hearty pasta. We love the combination of roasted cherry tomatoes and asparagus, Parmesan and pecorino cheeses and several fresh herbs.

---

3 tablespoons good quality olive oil
1 pint cherry tomatoes
8 ounces shitake mushrooms, stems removed and sliced
1 bunch asparagus, trimmed and cut into 2-inch pieces
8 garlic cloves, minced or grated
1 cup fresh sweet peas
1 medium zucchini, sliced
1 yellow crookneck squash, sliced
1 tablespoon freshly squeezed lemon juice
½ cup sun-dried tomatoes in oil, drained
½ cup freshly chopped basil
¾ pound linguine, cooked and drained
½ cup freshly grated Parmesan cheese

Preheat the oven to 425°F. Place the cherry tomatoes on a baking sheet, drizzle with 1 tablespoon of olive oil and season with salt and pepper. Roast the tomatoes for 15 minutes or until they begin to burst.

Meanwhile, combine the remaining 2 tablespoons of olive oil with the butter in a 3-quart pot. Add the mushrooms and asparagus and sauté, stirring often, for 5 minutes. Add the zucchini and yellow squash and sauté 2 minutes more. Add the garlic and peas and sauté 1 minute more. Stir in the lemon juice, sun-dried tomatoes, basil and the cooked pasta and stir to combine. Finish with Parmesan cheese.

PUMPKIN RICOTTA FARFALLE

SERVES 6

The kids will love this for Halloween and in the Fall. A quick bake that creates a hearty and satisfying pot of pasta...cook the pasta and mix everything together. Serve hot Italian sausages on the side for the grown-ups and enjoy your evening.

	Good quality olive oil
1	15-ounce container ricotta
1	15-ounce can pumpkin purée
2	large eggs, beaten
½	cup plain Greek yogurt
½	teaspoon ground nutmeg
½	teaspoon ground ginger
¾	pound farfalle pasta, cooked and drained
½	cup pecans, roughly chopped
2	tablespoons finely chopped fresh sage
2	garlic cloves, minced or grated
¾	cup grated Parmesan cheese
	Salt and freshly ground black pepper

Preheat the oven to 375°F. Lightly oil a 3-quart casserole with olive oil.

In a mixing large bowl, whisk together the ricotta, pumpkin purée, eggs, and Greek yogurt. Add the nutmeg and ginger and season liberally with slat and pepper. Mix well. Stir the cooked pasta into the cheese mixture to coat completely. Add the pecans, sage, garlic and ½ cup of the Parmesan cheese.

Spoon the pasta into the oiled casserole and top with the remaining Parmesan cheese. Bake uncovered for 30 minutes or until golden brown and heated through. Let stand for 5 minutes before serving.

TORTELLINI with
PEARS and GORGONZOLA

SERVES 4

Store-bought cheese tortellini with a Gorgonzola cream sauce and pears is either a first course or a light dinner. Use ripe red Bartlett or red Anjou pears for great flavor. This is heaven on a plate!

2 cups heavy whipping cream
3 garlic cloves, minced
¼ teaspoon red pepper flakes
2 large red-skinned pears – halved, cored and cut into ½-inch dice
5 ounces crumbled Gorgonzola cheese
2 9-ounce packages store-bought cheese tortellini
1 teaspoon fresh thyme, finely chopped
1 teaspoon fresh rosemary, finely chopped
½ cup chopped walnuts, toasted
  Salt and freshly ground pepper
  Freshly chopped chives

In a large, high-sided saucepan, place the cream, garlic and red pepper flakes. Bring to a boil over medium heat and cook for 5 minutes, stirring constantly to prevent the cream from boiling over. Reduce the heat to medium and cook for 10 minutes longer, stirring often, until the mixture has thickened. Add the pears and Gorgonzola cheese and mix gently. Remove from the heat and set aside.

Cook the tortellini in boiling, salted water according to the package directions. Reheat the sauce, stirring constantly, to heat the sauce through. Add the tortellini to the sauce along with the thyme, rosemary and walnuts. Season to taste with salt and pepper. Finish with chives.

WILD MUSHROOM RISOTTO

SERVES 4

If you have vegetarians at the table, this is the perfect main dish. It's not difficult to make risotto...just a bit time consuming because of the stirring...but it's worth it! The cremini, shitake, oyster mushroom combination is our favorite or use a package of dried wild mushrooms that you rehydrate in hot water for an earthy, wintry feel. Drizzle a little white truffle oil for an over-the-top finish.

8 cups low-sodium chicken broth or vegetable broth
2 tablespoons good quality olive oil
3 tablespoons unsalted butter
2 shallots, finely chopped
2 cups Arborio rice
1 cup dry white wine
1 tablespoon unsalted butter
Zest of one lemon
½ cup grated Parmesan cheese

¼ cup freshly chopped parsley
Salt and freshly ground pepper, to taste

For the Mushrooms

2 tablespoons unsalted butter
1 tablespoon good quality olive oil
1 pound assorted mushrooms (such as oyster, crimini or shiitake), sliced

Bring the broth to a boil in a 3-quart pot and keep hot.

Heat the olive oil with 2 tablespoons of the butter in another 3-quart pot over medium heat. Add the shallots and sauté, stirring often, until tender, about 3 minutes. Add the rice and cook to toast the rice, about 5 minutes. Add the white wine and stir until the wine has evaporated.

Ladle in 1 cup of simmering broth and cook at a strong simmer, stirring constantly, until absorbed. Continue adding broth, about ½ cup at a time, stirring frequently and letting each addition of broth absorb before adding the next. Cook until the rice is tender and creamy, about 15 to 20 minutes. Season the risotto with salt and pepper to taste.

For the Mushrooms: Heat the butter and olive oil in a 3-quart pot over high heat. Add the mushrooms and sauté until golden brown, about 5 minutes. Season with salt and pepper.

Remove the risotto from the heat and stir in the remaining tablespoon of butter, the lemon zest and the Parmesan cheese. Serve the risotto topped with the sautéed mushrooms and finish with chopped parsley.

ITALIAN SUNDAY GRAVY

SERVES 4

This is your go-to easy meat sauce. When you need to put dinner on the table in under an hour, this is the sauce to turn to. It has that rich, long-cooked flavor with plenty of garlic, dried oregano and red pepper flakes. The tomato paste adds a concentrated, long cooking flavor. Reserving some of the pasta water is ideal for adjusting the consistency of the sauce. We love to "fare la scarpetta"...mop up the wonderful sauce with a piece of bread!

2   tablespoons unsalted butter
2   tablespoons good quality olive oil
1   small sweet yellow onion, diced
1   carrot, grated
2   garlic cloves, minced or grated
1   generous pinch of red pepper flakes
1   teaspoon dried oregano
1   pound lean ground beef
1   28-ounce can diced tomatoes in juice
3   tablespoons tomato paste
½   cup whole milk
1   fresh basil sprig
    Salt and freshly ground pepper

Heat the butter and oil in a 3-quart pot over medium heat. Add the onion and carrot and sauté, stirring often, until the onion is tender and beginning to caramelize, about 10 minutes. Add the garlic, red pepper flakes and oregano and cook 1 minute more. Add the ground beef and cook, breaking up the meat, for 5 minutes.

Add the tomatoes and the juice, tomato paste, milk and the basil sprig and season with salt and pepper. Simmer 20 minutes.

The sauce can be refrigerated for up to 1 week. Reheat gently before serving.

PAELLA RICE

SERVES 4

This paella rice is as authentic as it can be in 30 minutes! A simple chicken and seafood rice that is healthy and vibrant. Add chorizo or any of the ingredients you have on hand to create a recipe that pleases you. You can vary the quantities of chicken, seafood and vegetables and add a cup of white wine for more liquid. A taste of the Mediterranean in a quick weeknight meal.

---

2   boneless skinless chicken breasts
2   tablespoons good quality olive oil
1   teaspoon smoked paprika
1   small sweet yellow onion, diced
1   clove garlic, minced or grated
½   pound Spanish chorizo
1   red bell pepper, seeded and diced
2   cups Bomba, Calasparra, Arborio or another short grain rice

½   teaspoon ground turmeric
3 ½   cups low-sodium chicken broth
8   medium raw shrimp, cleaned and deveined
8   raw mussels in shells, scrubbed and debearded
Salt and freshly ground pepper
Freshly chopped parsley

Cut the chicken into ½-inch strips. Season the chicken with the smoked paprika, salt and pepper.

In a 3-quart pot, heat the olive oil over medium heat. Add the onion and cook for 5 minutes, stirring often. Add the garlic and cook 1 minute more. Add the chorizo and bell pepper and cook for 3 minutes, stirring. Add the chicken and sauté, stirring often for 3 minutes. Add the rice, turmeric and salt and pepper and mix well. Add the chicken broth and bring the mixture to a boil. Reduce the heat to low, cover and cook for 20 minutes.

Remove the lid and add the shrimp and mussels to the top of the rice. Replace the lid and cook for 5 minutes more over low heat. Finish with parsley.

SPANISH RICE with PIQUILLO PEPPERS

SERVES 4

Spanish rice is essentially a rice pilaf, but with Spanish or Mexican flavors. The browning of the rice is essential to the nutty, almost toasty flavor of the rice. Be sure to fluff with a fork before serving. Spanish Piquillo peppers are easily found in a jar or can in most grocery stores. They have no heat and are thinner, sweeter and more delicate than a roasted red bell pepper.

- 6 tablespoons good quality olive oil
- 1 small sweet yellow onion, finely chopped
- 6 garlic cloves, minced or grated
- 6 tablespoons freshly chopped parsley
- 2 cups Valencia or Arborio rice
- 1 cup diced tomatoes, drained
- ½ cup roasted piquillo peppers or roasted red peppers, cut into thin strips
- 1 teaspoon smoked paprika
- ½ teaspoon ground turmeric
- 3 ½ cups low-sodium chicken broth
- ½ cup dry white wine
  Salt and freshly ground pepper

Heat the oil in a 3-quart pot over medium heat and sauté the onion until tender, about 5 minutes. Add the garlic and parsley and sauté for 1 minute more. Add the rice and sauté for 3 minutes, stirring often. Add the diced tomatoes, piquillo peppers, smoked paprika, turmeric, broth, wine and salt and pepper and bring the mixture to a boil. Cover the pot, reduce the heat to a simmer and cook over low heat for 20 minutes or until the rice is cooked through. Fluff with a fork.

CHEF'S TIP: The best tip for perfect rice is this...when the rice is finished cooking, carefully remove the lid and place a clean kitchen towel over the top of the pot. Replace the lid and wait 5 minutes. The towel will absorb any additional moisture from the rice and leave you with fluffy, perfect rice every time!

QUINOA with CUCUMBER, TOMATOES, MINT and FETA

SERVES 6 TO 8

We love the protein packed Mediterranean grain that is quinoa! Combined with fresh-from-the-garden flavors, you have something wonderfully healthy and so delicious. Substitute goat cheese for the feta and use your vegetable peeler to add shaved ribbons of additional veggies, if you like.

---

1 ½ cups red or traditional quinoa, rinsed
4 cups water
1 whole garlic clove, peeled
2 tablespoons fresh lemon juice
½ teaspoon Dijon mustard
½ cup good quality olive oil
½ cup chopped flat-leaf parsley

½ cup chopped fresh mint
2 Persian (baby) cucumbers, diced
1 pint sweet cherry tomatoes, halved
4 ounces Feta cheese, crumbled
2 green onions, chopped
Salt and freshly ground white pepper

Combine the rinsed quinoa, the garlic clove and ½ teaspoon salt with the water in a 3-quart pot over high heat. Bring to a boil, then reduce the heat to low, cover and simmer until the quinoa is tender, about 15 minutes. Drain well and return the quinoa to the pot.

Meanwhile, whisk together the lemon juice and mustard in a small bowl. Gradually whisk in the olive oil. Add the parsley and mint and season with salt and pepper.

While the quinoa is still warm, mix in ¼ cup of the dressing. Add the cucumber, tomatoes, crumbled feta and green onions and toss well. Add more dressing, if needed. Serve warm or cold.

WARNING: Hot Surface

SOMETHING SWEET

LANA'S DEEP DARK CHOCOLATE PUDDING CAKE

SERVES 6

This fudgy dessert is baked and served directly from your 3-quart pot! This pudding-like cake is sweet and luscious and best eaten warm with a spoon. Use a good quality unsweetened cocoa powder for this rich and decadent dessert. Serve with a scoop of vanilla ice cream and a few berries.

1	cup granulated sugar
1 ½	cups all-purpose flour
¾	cup high quality unsweetened cocoa powder
1 ½	teaspoons baking soda
1 ½	teaspoons baking powder
½	teaspoon salt
2	large eggs
1	cup whole milk
½	cup vegetable oil
1	teaspoon pure vanilla extract
1	cup boiling water

For the Frosting:

2	tablespoons unsalted butter
¾	cup semisweet chocolate chips
6	tablespoons heavy cream
1	cup confectioners' sugar, sifted
1	teaspoon pure vanilla extract
1	teaspoon espresso powder or instant coffee

In a mixing bowl, combine the sugar, flour, cocoa, baking soda, baking powder and salt. In a separate mixing bowl, whisk together the eggs, milk, oil and vanilla. Add the wet ingredients to the dry ingredients and whisk to combine. Add the boiling water and mix well.

Spray or butter a 3-quart pot and pour in the batter. Place the lid on the pot and cook the cake on your triple burner, on number 3 on the dial, for 1 hour. Remove the pot from the heat and let the cake stand, with the lid on, for 30 minutes more, to finish cooking.

For the frosting, place all of the ingredients in a saucepot over low heat. Whisk until smooth. Spread on the cake while the frosting is still warm.

BIRTHDAY CAKE in a POT

SERVES 6

We love this cake baked in a pot! The mascarpone cheese adds rich flavor to a store-bought cake mix and the sprinkles make it so festive.

We scoop the cake out of the pot into serving bowls and continue the celebration with sweet strawberry sauce and fluffy whipped cream.

- 8 ounces mascarpone cheese (about 1 cup), softened
- 2 egg whites
- ¼ cup vegetable oil
- 1 box yellow cake mix
- 1 cup water
- 4 tablespoons colored sprinkles

For the Strawberry Sauce

- ⅓ cup frozen strawberries, thawed and drained
- 2 ½ cups powdered sugar
  Whipped cream

Preheat the oven to 350°F. Butter a 3-quart pot.

Combine the mascarpone cheese, egg whites and vegetable oil in the bowl of your electric mixer. Beat on medium speed until well combined and creamy. Add the cake mix and water and mix until smooth, about 3 minutes. By hand, fold 3 tablespoons of the sprinkles into the cake batter. Pour the batter into the prepared pan and sprinkle the remaining sprinkles on top. Cover the pan with a lid and bake for 35 minutes. Remove the lid and bake for 10 minutes more, or until golden brown on top and a cake tester comes out clean.

Remove the cake from the oven, place the lid back on the pot and let the cake rest for 10 minutes.

Meanwhile, purée the strawberries with the powdered sugar in a blender or food processor.

Spoon the cake from the pot into serving bowls and top with the strawberry sauce and a dollop of whipped cream.

BLUEBERRY RICOTTA CAKE

SERVES 6

Just plain wonderful...delicious, light and luscious. A perfect everyday cake to serve with morning coffee or as a dessert. Add the zest of one lemon and the juice of one half lemon for a delightful lemon flavor or use any type of berry or even chocolate chips! Add fresh berries on the plate and whipped cream or drizzle on a little lemon-powdered sugar glaze.

---

1 ½   cups all-purpose flour
1   cup granulated sugar
2   teaspoons baking powder
½   teaspoon kosher salt
3   large eggs, at room temperature
1 ½   cups ricotta cheese
1   teaspoon pure vanilla extract
8   tablespoons (1 stick) unsalted butter, melted
1 ½   cups blueberries, raspberries or blackberries

Preheat oven to 350°F. Lightly coat a 3-quart pot with nonstick cooking spray.

Whisk together the flour, sugar, baking powder and salt in a mixing bowl.

In a separate bowl, whisk together the eggs, ricotta and vanilla until smooth. Fold in the dry ingredients until just blended. Then add the melted butter and fold gently. Fold in three-quarters of the berries, taking care not to crush them.

Pour the batter into the pot and scatter the remaining berries over the top. Place the lid on the pot and bake the cake, covered, for 40 minutes. Remove the lid and bake for another 15 minutes or until the cake is golden brown and a cake tester or toothpick comes out clean, approximately 50 to 60 minutes total. Let cool for 10 minutes before turning the cake out onto a plate.

CROISSANT BREAD PUDDING

SERVES 6

Think bread pudding, only so much more! The buttery flakiness of the croissants creates the wonderful texture. Use brown sugar instead of white sugar for a more caramelized flavor. Easy to make and out of this world delicious.

12 croissants
1 cup half & half
1 cup heavy whipping cream
½ cup granulated sugar
4 eggs
1 teaspoon pure vanilla extract
¼ teaspoon almond extract
¼ teaspoon salt
3 ounces almond paste, grated

Preheat the oven to 350°F. Butter a 3-quart pot. Tear the croissants into 2-inch pieces and place them in the pot.

In a mixing bowl, whisk together the half and half, cream, sugar, eggs, vanilla, almond extract and salt. Stir in the grated almond paste. Pour the egg mixture over the croissants and press down to allow the croissants to absorb the liquid. Let stand for 10 minutes.

Cover the saucepot with a lid or aluminum foil and bake for 30 minutes. Remove the lid and bake uncovered 15 minutes more, or until the croissants are puffy and golden brown.

COCONUT RICE PUDDING

SERVES 6

Comfort food to the max! Serve the rice pudding warm, topped with summer fruits or slice a mango to create alternate layers of fruit and warm pudding. It's simple and satisfying and you can dress it up with nuts, raisins, a dash of cinnamon or dried fruit.

- 2   **14-ounce cans unsweetened coconut milk**
- 2   **cups whole milk**
- ⅔   **cup granulated sugar**
- 1   **cup long-grain rice**
  Pinch of salt
- 1   **teaspoon pure vanilla extract**
  Whipped cream, for serving

Combine the coconut milk, whole milk, sugar, rice and salt in a 3-quart pot over medium heat and bring to a simmer. Adjust the heat so that the mixture is barely simmering and cook until the rice pudding is thick and silky, stirring often, about 40 minutes. Turn off the heat and stir in the vanilla.

Serve warm, with a dollop of whipped cream, or spoon into ramekins and chill.

CHOCOLATE PEANUT BUTTER CARAMEL CORN

MAKES 8 CUPS

This sweet and salty caramel corn is very addictive. Use peanut butter pretzels or your favorite pretzel and buy store bought popcorn for this scrumptious snack.

- 8 cups store-bought popcorn
- 1 cup honey roasted peanuts
- ½ cup packed dark brown sugar
- ½ cup light corn syrup
- 3 tablespoons unsalted butter
- ½ teaspoon salt
- ½ cup creamy peanut butter
- 1 teaspoon pure vanilla extract
- 1 cup coarsely chopped chocolate covered pretzels

Preheat the oven to 250°F. Line a large baking pan with aluminum foil and spray it lightly with non-stick cooking spray.

Combine the popcorn and peanuts in a large mixing bowl.

In a 3-quart pot, combine the brown sugar, corn syrup, butter and salt and bring to a boil over medium-high heat. Continue to boil, stirring occasionally, for 3 minutes. Remove the pan from the heat and stir in the peanut butter until completely melted. Stir in the vanilla.

Pour half of the caramel over the popcorn, tossing it with a wooden spoon. (Be careful, the bowl will get hot.) Continue adding the caramel until the popcorn is completely coated. Spread the mixture onto the prepared pan and bake for 20 minutes, stirring it after 10 minutes, then again after 20 minutes of baking. Sprinkle the chopped pretzels over the popcorn and bake for another 10 minutes. Stir until blended. Cool completely and eat.

BUTTERSCOTCH BUDINO

SERVES 6

Delight your friends and family with this uncomplicated and nostalgic dessert. It's unexpected and downright delicious! This indulgent Italian Budino (pudding) will become your go-to recipe for homemade pudding. Top each bowl with a dollop of whipped cream or add one tablespoon of sour cream when you are whipping cream for a tart, tangy flavor.

---

2   cups packed dark brown sugar
½   cup cornstarch
    Generous pinch of salt
4   large eggs, beaten
4   cups whole milk
2   teaspoons pure vanilla extract
6   tablespoons cold unsalted butter
⅓   cup dark Rum

Sift together the brown sugar, cornstarch and salt. Place the sifted mixture in a 3-quart pot. Add the beaten eggs and milk and whisk to combine.

Place the pot over medium heat and bring to a simmer, whisking constantly. Cook until the mixture thickens enough to coat the back of a spoon, about 5 minutes. Remove the pot from the heat and whisk in the vanilla, butter and dark Rum.

Serve the pudding warm or spoon it into ramekins and chill before serving.

AUTUMN APPLE ALMOND CRISP

SERVES 6

When you are dreaming of apple pie but don't have the time, an easy apple crisp is the next best thing. This comforting dessert of bubbling apples with a crunchy, sweet topping is perfect for your next tailgate or your holiday table.

For the Topping

- 1 ½ cups all-purpose flour
- 1 ⅛ cups old-fashioned oats
- 1 ⅛ cups dark brown sugar
- 1 ½ cups almonds, toasted and finely chopped
- 1 teaspoon ground cinnamon
  Pinch of salt
- 4 ounces (1 stick) cold unsalted butter, cut into ½-inch cubes

For the Filling

- 4 pounds sweet-tart apples (Gala, Fuji or Honey Crisp work well)
- 2 tablespoons fresh lemon juice
- 2 tablespoons all-purpose flour

Preheat the oven to 375°F. Butter a 3-quart pot.

To make the topping, place the flour, oats, brown sugar, almonds, cinnamon and cinnamon in a food processor and pulse until combined. Add the butter pieces and pulse a few times, just until the mixture resembles coarse crumbs.

Peel and core the apples and cut into ¼-inch-thick wedges and place them in a mixing bowl. Add the lemon juice, granulated sugar and flour and toss to combine. Transfer the apples to the prepared pan.

Crumble the oat topping evenly over the apple mixture and bake the crisp until the topping is golden and the apples are tender, about 45 minutes. Serve warm.

MILK CHOCOLATE ALMOND BREAD PUDDING with SEA SALT CARAMEL SAUCE

SERVES 6

This is a definite crowd pleaser and the kids will love it. This steamy, fluffy bread pudding is the never-fail solution to making any day better! And, when you stir in chocolate milk it makes it 10-times better! For the beginner cook, use frozen French toast, defrosted, and cut into 2-inch cubes. Serve with a drizzle of sea salt caramel sauce and a dollop of whipped cream.

1	1-pound loaf day-old bread, cut into 1-inch cubes (Brioche, challah, egg bread or Hawaiian Bread work well)	3	large eggs
		1 ¼	cups granulated sugar
		1	teaspoon almond extract
		1	cup mini chocolate chips
4	cups chocolate milk	½	cup sliced almonds

Preheat the oven to 350°F. Butter a 3-quart pot.

In a large mixing bowl, pour the chocolate milk over the bread cubes and let stand for 20 minutes or up to 1 hour.

In a separate bowl, whisk together the eggs, sugar and almond extract. Stir the mixture into the soaked bread and fold in the chocolate chips. Pour the mixture, with all of the liquid, into the prepared saucepot and top with the sliced almonds.

Place the lid on the pot and bake the bread pudding for 45 minutes. Remove the lid and bake until golden brown and set, 20 to 30 minutes more.

(CONTINUED ON NEXT PAGE)

SEA SALT CARAMEL SAUCE MAKES 2 CUPS

16 tablespoons (2 sticks) unsalted butter

1 ½ cups packed dark brown sugar

1 cup heavy whipping cream

3 liberal pinches of sea salt

Combine all of the ingredients in a saucepan and bring to a boil over high heat. Reduce the heat to low and simmer for 5 minutes. Cool to thicken.

HOLIDAY CRANBERRY APPLE CRUMBLE

SERVES 6

Celebrate the Fall and holiday season with this warm and comforting divine dessert. The sweetness of the topping in contrast to the tartness of the cranberries makes this warming dessert so satisfying. The best apples to use are Granny Smith, Honey Crisp and Empire...or mix all three! Your house will smell ridiculously delicious.

2 cups fresh or frozen cranberries, thawed
4 large green apples – peeled, cored and sliced
1 cup granulated sugar
Zest and juice of 1 lemon
¾ teaspoon ground cinnamon
¼ teaspoon ground nutmeg

For the Cream Cheese Filling:

4 ounces cream cheese, at room temperature
2 tablespoons granulated sugar

For the Topping:

¾ cup sifted all-purpose flour
¾ cup packed dark brown sugar
¾ cup old-fashioned oats
Pinch of salt
12 tablespoons (1 ½ sticks) cold unsalted butter, cut into small pieces
¾ cup pecans, chopped
Vanilla ice cream

Preheat the oven to 350°F. Butter a 3-quart pot. Combine the cranberries and apple slices in a large mixing bowl. Add the sugar, lemon zest, lemon juice, cinnamon and nutmeg and mix well. Pour the fruit mixture into the prepared saucepot.

For the cream cheese filling, in a small mixing bowl, combine the cream cheese and the 2 tablespoons of granulated sugar. Drop by dollops over the fruit mixture.

To make the topping, combine the flour, brown sugar, oats and salt in a food processor and pulse until combined. Add the butter and pulse a few times, just until the mixture resembles coarse crumbs. Remove the mixture from the food processor and stir in the pecans. Spoon the topping over the fruit.

Bake until juices bubble and the topping is golden brown, about 35 to 40 minutes. Serve warm (even better with ice cream).

BERRY BALSAMIC CRISP

SERVES 6

If you love berries like we do, this one is for you. Add the complexity of balsamic vinegar, which plays beautifully against the sweetness of the berries, to form a perfect union of flavors. Use any blend of berries you prefer or try a mix of berries with slices of stone fruit. To truly impress, reduce a ½ cup of balsamic in a small saucepan for about 5 to 6 minutes and let it cool and thicken. Serve with vanilla ice cream and drizzle the balsamic reduction on top.

For the Berries:

- 2 cups strawberries, sliced
- 1 cup blackberries
- 1 cup blueberries
- 1 cup raspberries
- 6 tablespoons granulated sugar
- 2 tablespoons balsamic vinegar

For the Topping:

- ½ cup pecans or walnuts, toasted and roughly chopped
- ⅔ cup all-purpose flour
- ⅓ cup dark brown sugar
- ⅓ cup granulated sugar
- 8 tablespoons (1 stick) cold unsalted butter, cut into small pieces
  Freshly Whipped Cream

Preheat the oven to 375°F. Combine the berries with the sugar, balsamic vinegar and cornstarch in a 3-quart pot. Place the pan over medium heat and cook gently, until the juices begin to run from the berries, about 5 minutes. Remove from the heat and set aside.

To make the topping, place half of the nuts, flour, brown sugar and granulated sugar in a food processor and pulse until combined. Add the butter and pulse a few times, just until the mixture resembles coarse crumbs. Remove the mixture from the food processor and stir in the remaining nuts.

Sprinkle the topping evenly over the berries and bake until the topping is lightly browned and the berries are bubbling, about 35-40 minutes. Serve warm. Even better with ice cream.

BANANAS FOSTER

SERVES 4

The historic New Orleans' restaurant Brennan's claims the invention of Bananas Foster. In the 1950s, New Orleans was the major port of entry for bananas shipped from Central and South America and restaurant owner Owen Brennan challenged his chef to make something interesting with the fruit. Bananas Foster was an immediate hit and Brennan's continues to serve tens of thousands of pounds of it each year. In our houses, Bananas Foster also doubles as a perfect topping for French Toast!

- 8 tablespoons (1 stick) unsalted butter
- 1 cup packed dark brown sugar
- 6 small bananas – peeled, halved and sliced lengthwise
- ½ cup banana liqueur or dark Rum
- ½ teaspoon ground cinnamon

Melt the butter in a 3-quart pot over medium-low heat. Add the brown sugar and cook the mixture until the sugar dissolves, about 3 minutes. Add the bananas and cook for 2 minutes on each side, until just tender, turning once.

Remove the pan from the heat and add the banana liqueur or Rum. Use a long lighter to ignite the mixture. Place the pot back on the heat and simmer the mixture until the flame dies out.

PEARS POACHED in RED WINE
with MASCARPONE CREAM

SERVES 4

The classic French approach to poaching fruit by slowly simmering in wine and spices turns any variety of pears into a luscious and elegant ending to a meal. The aromatics of star anise and ginger along with cinnamon and citrus zest add a new level of taste. Simmering the poaching liquid to create a sauce adds a huge boost of flavor to the dessert.

For the Pears

- 4 firm ripe pears
- 1 750 ml. bottle dry red wine (Beaujolais or Pinot Noir works well)
- ¾ cup granulated sugar
- 1 tablespoon vanilla paste
- 3 whole cloves
- 3 1-inch long strips of fresh orange zest
- 1 1-inch piece of fresh ginger, peeled
- 1 cinnamon stick

For the Mascarpone Cream

- ½ cup heavy whipping cream
- ½ cup mascarpone cheese
- 2 tablespoons confectioners sugar

Combine the wine, sugar, vanilla paste, cloves, orange zest, ginger and cinnamon stick in a 3-quart saucepot. Bring the mixture to a simmer.

Peel the pears, leaving the stems intact, and cut a ½ inch off of the bottom of each pear to create a flat bottom. Place the pears in the poaching liquid. Let them simmer gently for about 15 minutes, then begin testing them with the tip of a small paring knife. Remove one pear and gently poke the knife into the bottom of the pear. The pear should be tender throughout. Cooking times will vary from 15 to 20 minutes, depending on the ripeness, size and variety of the pears.

Remove the pears from the poaching liquid and let them cool.

Place the poaching liquid back on the burner and simmer until reduced by half or until thickened.

To make the Mascarpone Whipped Cream, whip the cream in a cold bowl with chilled beaters until fairly thick. Stop the mixer and add the mascarpone and sugar to the bowl. Continue whipping until thick.

CLASSIC + CHERRIES
+ JUBILEE

SERVES 6

This elegant holiday dessert is wonderful for entertaining and is sure to impress your guests. A vintage recipe from the 1960s that deserves a comeback. When you flambé the sweet dark cherries with the Kirsch, a cherry liqueur, it makes it a special celebration. It has that wow-factor! You can use either fresh pitted cherries, frozen cherries or jarred or canned cherries, packed in juice.

16 ounces canned pitted sour cherries, with their juice
½ cup granulated sugar
2 tablespoons freshly grated orange zest
1 tablespoon cornstarch
⅓ cup Kirsch or Cognac
1 pint vanilla ice cream
Chocolate shavings

Drain the cherries, reserving the juice. Measure the juice and add enough water to measure 1 ½ cups of liquid. Pour the liquid into a 3-quart pot and add the sugar and orange zest. Bring the mixture to a boil, reduce the heat and simmer, uncovered, for 10 minutes.

Place the cornstarch in a small mixing bowl. Remove 2 tablespoons of the cherry liquid from the pot and add it to the cornstarch. Stir the mixture to dissolve. Gradually stir the cornstarch mixture into the liquid in the pot. Simmer, stirring constantly until thickened, about 2 minutes. Add the cherries and stir to combine.

Remove the pan from the heat and add the Kirsch. Use a long lighter to ignite the mixture. Place the pot back on the heat and simmer the mixture until the flame dies out.

Divide the ice cream among six bowls. Spoon the sauce over the ice cream and finish with chocolate shavings.

DRINKS

+

SIPS

SWEET & SPICY MARGARITAS
with CANDIED JALAPEÑOS

MAKES 4 MARGARITAS

This sweet and spicy sip is a wonderful version of the popular cocktail. Muddle the jalapeños and lime juice to begin this fantastic drink, then pour over ice into salt or sugar rimmed glass and garnish with the candied jalapeños. Store the candied jalapeños in mason jars in the refrigerator to use on tacos, short ribs, as a sandwich condiment or a guacamole ingredient. Cheers!

---

4   thin slices fresh jalapeño
¼   cup freshly squeezed lime juice
1   cup good quality Tequila
1   cup pineapple juice
4   ounces agave nectar

In a large cocktail shaker, muddle the jalapeño slices with the lime juice. Fill the shaker with ice and add the Tequila, pineapple juice and agave nectar. Shake vigorously. Fill 4 glasses with fresh ice. Strain the margarita over the ice and finish with a few candied jalapeños.

CANDIED JALAPEÑOS MAKES 1 PINT

2   pounds jalapeño peppers
⅔   cup apple cider vinegar
2   cups granulated sugar
     Juice of 2 limes

Slice the jalapeño peppers into ¼-inch thick rounds. Combine the vinegar, sugar and lime juice in 3-quart pot. Bring to a boil over medium heat. Reduce the heat to low and simmer for 5 minutes. Add the jalapeños and simmer until the jalapeños are slightly wilted and darkened, about 3 minutes.

Using a slotted spoon, transfer the jalapeños to a 1-Pint mason jar. Return the syrup to a boil and cook for 5 minutes. Ladle the hot syrup over the jalapeños into the jar. Close the jar tightly and let cool, then store in the refrigerator for up to 2 months.

DECADENT HOT CHOCOLATE

SERVES 6

Infuse your favorite flavoring into this rich, creamy hot chocolate by adding a couple of drops of peppermint oil or orange oil or by spiking the cocoa with your favorite liqueur. We use Peppermint Schnapps at the holiday time, Kahlua on cold nights and Amaretto or Chambord when we want bold flavor.

- 6 **cups whole milk**
- 2 **cups half & half**
- ½ **cup high quality unsweetened cocoa powder**
- 4 **ounces bittersweet chocolate, chopped**
- 1 **cup granulated sugar**
- 1 **teaspoon pure vanilla extract**
  Lots of mini marshmallows

Combine the milk and half & half in a 3-quart pot and bring to a simmer over medium heat.

In a small mixing bowl, combine the cocoa powder, chopped chocolate and sugar. Add a few teaspoons of the hot milk mixture to the cocoa mixture and blend to make a paste. Scrape the paste into the saucepan with the remaining milk mixture and whisk until smooth. Simmer for 2 minutes. Stir in the vanilla and serve topped with lots of marshmallows.

SPIKED ROSEMARY APPLE CIDER

SERVES 6

This hot blend of apple cider and whiskey infused with rosemary and holiday spices is something you can keep warming on the stove all day for guests. The hot cider fills your home with the aroma of the holidays and the rosemary adds a hint of herbaceous flavor.

- 8 cups apple cider
- ¼ cup packed dark brown sugar
- 2 cinnamon sticks
- 8 whole cloves
- 3 sprigs fresh rosemary
- 1 cup Whiskey

Combine the apple cider, brown sugar, cinnamon sticks, cloves and rosemary in a 3-quart pot. Bring the mixture to a boil over medium heat, then reduce the heat to a simmer and cook for 10 minutes. Stir in the whiskey, strain and serve.

CHAI MAPLE CIDER

SERVES 6

Black tea is steeped in cider is one of our favorite winter drinks. The spices of chai make a perfect complement to warm apple cider. Using cider that is already spiced will yield an even spicier drink. Add a touch of rum or a spoonful of caramel and serve with a holiday brunch.

- 4 wide strips fresh orange peel
- 2 cinnamon sticks, broken in half
- 1-inch piece of fresh ginger, peeled and sliced
- 8 cloves, whole
- 3 cardamom pods
- 12 whole black peppercorns
- 4 cups apple cider
- 1 cup water
- ⅓ cup Grade B pure maple syrup
- 8 black tea bags
- Orange slices

Place the orange peel, ginger, broken cinnamon sticks, cloves, cardamom and peppercorns in the center of a 6-inch double-thick square of cheesecloth. Tie the bundle with kitchen string.

Combine the apple cider, water, maple syrup and the spice bundle. Bring to a boil and simmer for 10 minutes. Add the tea bags and cover the pot. Let stand for 10 minutes. Remove the tea bags and bring the cider back to a simmer.

Ladle into mugs and finish with orange slices.

NEW ORLEANS
CAFÉ BRULOT

SERVES 6

You will literally "light up the table" with this flaming coffee drink! Those who take their cocktails very seriously have been known to serve it at breakfast or brunch, referring to it as an "eye opener." This recipe is our favorite version of the classic and is especially delicious served with a dollop of whipped cream on top.

    Peel of 1 orange, cut into 1-inch strips
    Peel of 1 lemon, cut into 1-inch strips
6 tablespoons granulated sugar
2 cups Cognac or Kahlua
1 cup Grand Marnier or Cointreau
4 cups freshly brewed strong black coffee

Combine the orange peel, lemon peel, sugar, Cognac and Grand Marnier in a 3-quart pot and place over medium-low heat. Stir to dissolve the sugar. When the mixture is warm, remove the pot from the heat and ignite the alcohol with a long lighter. Return the pot to the heat and stirring gently, pour the coffee into the pot in a slow, thin stream, continuing to stir until the flame dies out. Ladle into cups and serve.

CRANBERRY MULLED WINE

MAKES ABOUT 8 CUPS

So very drinkable and comforting and especially festive around the holidays. Make a large batch ahead of time and add more to your pot to keep warm. Mulled wine has been warming people for centuries. Stay warm this winter with this delicious sip!

---

1   750-ml bottle light-bodied red wine
    (Beaujolais, Pinot Noir or Syrah)
1   cinnamon stick
1   1-inch piece of fresh ginger, peeled and sliced
2   oranges – peel left on, sliced and seeded
2   lemons – peel left on, sliced and seeded
1   cup granulated sugar
1   cup fresh cranberries
4   cups apple cider

Combine the wine, cinnamon stick, ginger, sliced oranges and lemons, sugar, cranberries and apple cider in a 3-quart pot. Bring to a slow simmer and cook for 30 minutes. Strain and serve in mugs.

INSPIRATIONAL MENU IDEAS
for your TRIPLE BURNER BUFFET

The following menus have been seen on HSN over the years. Consider making your own signature dishes, or order take-out from your favorite restaurant, and fill your triple burner for a party anytime!

LAZY SUNDAY MORNING BRUNCH
Scrambled Eggs with Green Chiles
    and Jack Cheese
Canadian Bacon
Jalapeño Hash Browns

THAI FEAST
Chicken Satay
Thai Yellow Rice
Spring Rolls in Chafer Insert

A SWEET ENDING
Peach Pecan Crisp
Warm Butterscotch Pudding
Chocolate Coconut Cream Fondue

TAKE A DIP
Reuben Dip
Caramelized Onion Dip
Warm Blue Cheese Dip

ITALIAN STATION
Penne with Gorgonzola Cream Sauce,
    Asparagus and Tomatoes
Cheese Ravioli in Pink Sauce
Meatballs in Red Sauce

HOLIDAY SIDE DISH BUFFET
Caramelized Brussels Sprouts
Sourdough Apple Stuffing
Whipped Sweet Potatoes with Praline
    Topping

A TRIBUTE TO THE SOUTH
Fried Chicken
Creamy Cheese Grits
Southern Greens with Bacon

HORS D'OEUVRES BUFFET
Mini Quiches
Swedish Meatballs
Honey Mustard Chicken Wings

A PERFECT PASTA BAR
Baked Rigatoni with Pancetta
Penne Puttanesca
Pesto Parmesan Tortellini
    with Blistered Cherry Tomatoes

SOUP BUFFET
Pumpkin Soup with
    Cinnamon Whipped Cream
Quick Clam Chowder
Smoky Split Pea Soup

FOOTBALL FIESTA
Chicken with Sautéed Onions
    and Peppers
Beer Braised Carnitas
Spanish Rice

SWEET ENDING
Cherries Jubilee
Apple Almond Cobbler
Berry Balsamic Crisp

CHINESE FOOD BUFFET
Sweet and Sour Pork
Vegetable Fried Rice
Crispy Egg Rolls

INDEX